(12)

$$\frac{S}{S-H}$$

D0854363

R 50453

P.J.

THE NEW TEMPLE SHAKESPEARE

Edited by M. R. Ridley, M.A.

HAMLET

by William Shakespeare

London: J. M. DENT & SONS LTD.
New York: E. P. DUTTON & CO. INC.

Editor's General Note

The Text. The editor has kept before him the aim of presenting to the modern reader the nearest possible approximation to what Shakespeare actually wrote. The text is therefore conservative, and is based on the earliest reliable printed text. But to avoid distraction (*a*) the spelling is modernised, and (*b*) a limited number of universally accepted emendations is admitted without comment. Where a Quarto text exists as well as the First Folio the passages which occur only in the Quarto are enclosed in square brackets [ ] and those which occur only in the Folio in brace brackets { }.

Scene Division. The rapid continuity of the Elizabethan curtainless production is lost by the 'traditional' scene divisions. Where there is an essential difference of place these scene divisions are retained. Where on the other hand the change of place is insignificant the scene division is indicated only by a space on the page. For ease of reference, however, the 'traditional' division is retained at the head of the page and in line numbering.

Notes. Passages on which there are notes are indicated by a † in the margin.

Punctuation adheres more closely than has been usual to the 'Elizabethan' punctuation of the early texts. It is often therefore more indicative of the way in which the lines were to be delivered than of their syntactical construction.

Glossaries are arranged on a somewhat novel principle, not alphabetically, but in the order in which the words or phrases occur. The editor is much indebted to Mr J. N. Bryson for his collaboration in the preparation of the glossaries.

v

Note

The text for this edition of the play was originally prepared, and the introduction written, before the appearance of Dr. Dover Wilson's brilliant and exhaustive study, *The Manuscript of Shakespeare's Hamlet*. Though I think that he is sometimes over-complicated, and though I should not accept all his conclusions, none the less any reader of his work will be as clear as I am myself that in my introduction I seriously over-simplified the problem of the relation of the Q2 and F texts. The considerable modifications that I should now wish to make are outside the scope of a reprinting, and must wait for a complete revision, but I am taking the opportunity of the present (1952) reprint to change a certain number of readings.

M. R. R.

Preface

The Text. In July of 1602 James Roberts the printer entered in the Stationers' Registers "A booke called *the Revenge of* HAMLETT *Prince ⟨of⟩ Denmarke as yt was latelie Acted by the Lord Chamberleyne his servantes.*" In the next year either Roberts was anticipated by some pirate, or (as seems more probable from the fact that " N. L." appears as publisher of both the First and Second Quartos) because Roberts and N. L. got impatient, there appeared the "First Quarto" of *Hamlet* with the title-page, "THE / Tragicall Historie of / HAMLET / *Prince of Denmarke* By William Shake-speare. / As it hath beene diuerse times acted by his Highnesse ser-/ uants in the Cittie of London: as also in the two V- / niuersities of Cambridge and Oxford, and else- where / At London printed for N. L. and Iohn Trundell. / 1603." There is no question that, whoever was responsible for the piracy, this is a pirated text. As illuminating the methods of pirates and also throwing light upon an intermediate stage in the development of *Hamlet* to the shape that we know this First Quarto is of great interest, but as any kind of authority for the received text of the play it is, except in a few isolated instances, quite valueless.

In 1604 appeared the "Second Quarto": "THE / Tragicall His-torie of / HAMLET, / *Prince of Denmarke.* / By William Shakespeare. / Newly imprinted and enlarged to almost as much / againe as it was, according to the true and perfect / Coppie. / AT LONDON, / Printed by I. R. for N. L. and are to be sold at his / shoppe vnder Saint Dunstons Church in / Fleetstreet. 1604." It is clear from the title-page that this was to be regarded as the authorised version and to oust its predecessor of the year before. It is on the whole

HAMLET

Hamlet as we know it, though there are marked differences between it and the Folio text, which we shall consider later.

The text of Hamlet in the Folio of 1623 corresponds on the whole very closely with the Second Quarto except in the matter of omissions and insertions. That is to say, where the two texts correspond they correspond more or less verbatim, and there is no evidence that the Folio is the result of anything like a detailed revision. Such verbal differences as there are are mainly matters of emendations of words or phrases which, one may suppose, the Folio editors found difficult or disliked ; and there is no evidence, nor I think any probability, that these alterations are due to Shakespeare himself. On the other hand there is a considerable number of passages of varying and sometimes considerable length which occur only in one or other of the texts. One may reasonably suppose that the passages which the Folio omits were cut out of the Quarto text for acting purposes, or in at least one case were omitted because they had by 1623 lost the piquancy of topical allusion. The passages which occur only in the Folio are more difficult to account for.

Various views have been taken with regard to the First Quarto. It is moderately clear that it is, at any rate in part, the result (as is common with piracies) of the taking down of the play in shorthand, certain deficiencies being filled out by the printer securing, by some presumably underhand means, one or two of the actors' parts. In this case, for example, all the speeches of Marcellus, as also a long speech of Voltimand in II. ii. 60-80 (the parts of Voltimand and Marcellus could obviously easily be doubled), are almost perfect. It would be easy to suppose that Q 1 is nothing but a shorthand transcript of the play in some stage or other of its development if it were not for one or two small points. The grave-digger, for example, is said in the stage directions of Q 1 to throw up a shovel, whereas what he obviously throws up is a skull, and no transcriber who had seen the play could make this particular error, though no doubt it is possible that the transcriber's note of skull was misread either from his shorthand or his script as shovel.[1] But the more difficult problem is " of what kind of version of the play is Q 1 a misrepresentation?" Not certainly of the finished version of Q 2, since in two salient particulars, quite apart from any question of verbal correspondence, the plots of Q 1 and Q 2 are different. In Q 1 the Queen is quite clearly innocent of all knowledge of her first husband's murder and after the revelation of it is definitely in alliance with Hamlet; and also the suggestion of the poisoned rapier and the poisoned cup both come from the King and neither from Laertes. And as a minor point, Polonius is called Corambis and Reynaldo is called Montano, a difference which is not accountable for by an error in hearing.

On the other hand it seems to me that Q 1 represents, or misrepresents, a state of the play much nearer to Q 2 than is sometimes supposed. In the first place, we should at least pay some small attention to the title-page of Q 2 which advertises itself as 'enlarged to almost as much againe as it was, according to the true and perfect Coppie.' Suppose that we knew nothing of vexed questions of old plays of *Hamlet* or lost plays of *Hamlet*. Suppose that we possessed a volume (Q 1) which advertised itself as 'The Tragicall Historie of Hamlet Prince of Denmarke, By William Shakespeare,' and stated moreover that the play had been diverse times acted both in London and in other places. We have not seen *Hamlet* acted, but we have seen other plays by this same dramatist, who

---

[1] Errors which suggest stenography are such things as *impudent* for *impotent*, *arganian* for *Hyrcanian*, and *calagulate* for *coagulate*. On the other hand such an error as *guise* for *gules* can hardly be auditory, nor *sawe* for *life*.

is recognised as at least one of the competent dramatists of the age. And whatever else we may have thought of his plays they have been obviously skilful and finished productions, and have contained a great deal of excellent poetry. This volume has filled us with equal degrees of surprise and disappointment. It seems oddly short, and for the most part rather staccato in movement. Every now and again we come on half a dozen lines that seem to have the ring of poetry that we have been accustomed to, but before we know where we are the verse has broken down into bad prose; and pretty frequently it is mere nonsense. And we conclude that no play in this shape, whether by Shakespeare or anyone else, was ever acted diverse times; and if we have had experience of other piracies, we have a good guess at what has happened. Next year appears another volume with exactly the same title, but stating that it is enlarged according to the true and perfect copy. Surely our natural supposition is that the true and perfect copy was there all the time, and that this volume represents it, whereas the former volume garbled it. And I believe that our natural supposition would be not far from the truth. One of the remarkable things about Q 1 is its astonishing inequality. A good deal of it not only resembles but exactly corresponds with Q 2 (sometimes, indeed, giving us the right reading where Q 2 falls into error); but where it does not correspond it much more often than not descends to stuff which not only could not have been written by Shakespeare, but which could not have been written by any Elizabethan dramatist nor delivered by any Elizabethan actor on the Elizabethan stage. Kyd and Marlowe and Peele and Greene at their poorest at least knew enough of the technique of their job to write lines that would scan. But what much of this stuff reads like, and I believe is, is not bad poetry, but fairly intelligent, though hopelessly dull, para-

phrase of good poetry.   There is no space here to illustrate this at
all convincingly.   I can give only one very brief instance.

> Queene. *Hamlet, thou cleaues my heart in twaine.*
> Ham.   *O throw away the worser part of it, and keepe the better.*

That surely is exactly the 'sense' of Q 2, but equally surely it is not
the rhythm of anything at all.   And similar instances could be
multiplied indefinitely.   I am not, of course, suggesting that Q 1 is
nothing but an incorrect representation of the text of Q 2.   Not
only do the differences in plot and in names already mentioned forbid
that supposition, but so also do a number of lines which, being
quite adequate verse, are presumably correctly reported, but to which
there is nothing at all correspondent in Q 2.   All I am suggesting is
that the *Hamlet* which in 1603 had been diverse times acted was a good
deal nearer the *Hamlet* we know (from Q 2), and needed less drastic
revision to bring it to its final form, than has usually been supposed.

It seems further that one should not entirely dismiss Q 1 in con-
sidering the text.   The unhappy stenographer, astonishing blunders
though he makes, mainly because he clearly was incompetent and
the actors' pace was frequently too much for him, so that, for example,
the famous ' To be or not to be' soliloquy appears in a shape
which it quite clearly never could have had in any version however immature, nevertheless was doing his best to put down what
he heard ; and when therefore we find that the result of his efforts
is represented as ' *beckles* ore his *bace*,' we should I think be cautious
in assuming that the Q 2 reading ' *bettles* ' is no more than an error
for the Folio reading ' *beetles*.'   That is to say that in constructing a
text which is to be as near as we can arrive to what Shakespeare
had finally written, we shall be wise to glance occasionally at Q 1
as a check.

HAMLET

The discussion of the exact way in which Q 1 came to be what it is is no doubt of speculative and bibliographical interest, but not, I think, of much intrinsic importance when we have Q 2 in front of us. But some examination of the differences between Q 2 and the Folio is of great interest and of real importance, not only as helping us to determine what Shakespeare's *Hamlet* was, but also as illuminating the general relations between the Folio text and the Quartos where they exist.

In the first place, then, there is a number of cases in which the Folio compositor has introduced new errors. We find, for example, *talkes* for *takes* (I. i. 163), *bak'd* for *bark'd* (I. v. 71), *cape* for *carp* (II. i. 62), *speed* for *heed* (II. i. 110), *cap* for *lap* (II. ii. 230), *valiant* for *valanct* (II. ii. 422), *surge* for *sugar* (III. i. 48), *pagan or Norman* for *pagan nor man* (III. ii. 33), *breath* for *brother* (III. iv. 65), *their corporall* for *the incorporall* (III. iv. 118), *politician* for *pelican* (IV. v. 144), *paeoncies* for *pansies* (IV. v. 174), *buy* for *lay* (IV. vii. 183), *sixteene* for *sexton* (V. i. 162), *sement* for *sequent* (V. ii. 54), *debate* for *defeat* (V. ii. 58), *mother* for *brother* (V. ii. 234). Now even in this brief list of illustrative examples one noteworthy point stands out. As a rule it is clear that the Folio compositor set from a Quarto where one existed, often from a Quarto that had been corrected, presumably in the playhouse, but at any rate from a printed text and not from MS. But there are at least two errors in the above list which look like errors made in setting from MS. rightly read by the compositor of Q 2 and wrongly by the compositor of F. A compositor would have to be astonishingly careless to read a printed *pelican* or a printed *the incorporall* (correctly spaced) as the Folio compositor read them, but he might easily have trouble with either if he was trying to decipher script.

Then there is a number of cases in which the Folio is pretty

certainly right in its correction of the Quarto; for example:
cou'nant for *comart* (I. i. 93), *good* for *coold* (I. ii. 77), *lust* for *but*
(I. v. 55), *warrant* for *wit* (II. i. 38), *watch* for *wath* (II. ii. 148), *thumb* for
the umber (III. ii. 353), *warrant* for *wait* (III. iv. 6), *pandars* for *pardons*
(III. iv. 88), *ayme* for *yawne* (IV. v. 9), *checking* for *the King* (IV. vii. 62),
shortly for *thirtie* (V. i. 299), and so on. None of these is beyond the
intelligence of anyone correcting the Quarto without reference to a
MS., though one or two of them, for example, *cou'nant*, the two
warrants (the errors, by the way, are interesting as showing Shakespeare's contracted form of the word which often causes trouble),
and *ayme* perhaps rather suggest that a MS. was handy.

Then we find, as invariably in the Folio, a large number of
alterations, some more or less indifferent, others, and these usually
enfeebling, where the Folio is apparently polishing up the Quarto
and making it more genteel. For example: (of the first class),
question for *speak to* (I. i. 45), *day* for *morne* (I. i. 150), *wafts* for
waues (I. iv. 61), *chamber* for *closet* (II. i. 76), *repulsed* for *repell'd*
(II. ii. 146), *waile* for *mourne* (II. ii. 151), *should be* for *shall grow*
(II. ii. 264), *burial* for *funeral* (IV. v. 210), *saylors* for *seafaring men*
(IV. vi. 2), *haste* for *speed* (IV. vi. 23); and (of the second class),
just for *jump* (I. i. 65), *to drink deep* for *for to drink* (I. ii. 175),
since not for *sith nor* (II. ii. 6), *why* for *swounds* (II. ii. 577), *pith*
for *pitch* (III. i. 86), *breathes* for *breakes* (III. ii. 383), *dangerous* for
neer's (III. iii. 6), *fresh* for *flush* (III. iii. 81), *past* for *topt* (IV. vii. 88),
doubts for *drownes* (IV. vii. 192), *hath lain* for *hath lyen you* (V. i. 173),
rites for *crants* (V. i. 233), *teach* for *learn* (V. ii. 9), and so on. It will
be noticed that almost none of these is a matter of the correct or incorrect reading of the same word, whether in MS. or print. These
are all definite alterations, whoever made them. (It is perhaps worth
mentioning that further and more notable instances of this same

tendency to substitute the more ordinary, and usually less vigorous, word for the less usual, will be found in the Folio of *King Lear* as well as in other plays.)

Finally, there are the insertions and omissions. Some of the Folio insertions are of course no more than further examples of the same process of tidying up the errors, or supposed errors, of the Quarto, whether in sense or metre. One of these is particularly interesting as showing almost beyond doubt that the Folio was set either from a MS. or with a MS. at hand to refer to, or from a copy of Q 2 that had been corrected from MS. If the reader who is interested will turn for a moment to V. i. 106 he will see what happened. The Quarto compositor had in front of him the passage as it stands ; he set correctly down to the first ' recoveries ' ; his eye was then caught by the second ' recoveries,' which he took to be the one he had just set (a common cause of omission), and he went cheerfully on ' to have his fine pate.' The Folio puts the muddle right, but probably not by just a bit of extempore patching, but by reference to the original. The same is probably true of III. ii. 115-6 and V. i. 35-8.

But leaving aside these remedial insertions, we have others of a different significance. In the first place, a good deal of Hamlet's often-noted trick of verbal repetition is given him by Folio only. Perhaps the trick was found to be effective in the early performances and so additional examples of it were subsequently introduced. At any rate these are almost certainly real insertions, and not mere remedying of Q 2's omissions. And the same is true of two long passages which occur only in F, II. ii. 240-70 and 338-61. The first of these is the most significant of all the ' insertions.' It is difficult to imagine how the Quarto compositor omitted it if he ever had it in front of him (unless indeed he somehow missed an entire page; but the length of the passage is inadequate for one of Shakespeare's ordinary pages where we can test their length), and equally difficult to imagine that it is not Shakespeare's own work. If so, it seems hard to escape from the conclusion that here at least we have a definite later addition by Shakespeare himself; though on the whole one would like to escape, since the passage, though well enough as a whole, and with one or two famous phrases in it, is of no particular dramatic value, and is indeed oddly like the passages which, as we shall see later, the Folio omits rather than inserts. Some seventy lines later is another passage, which occurs only in the Folio, but this is of a different and topical character, and it is fairly clear that its omission from the Quarto or its insertion in the Folio (probably the latter) is due to its topicality. It should perhaps be pointed out for what little it is worth that there is a slight (far from decisive) typographical indication of dislocation in the Quarto text immediately after the second 'omission,' that the two passages are of roughly equivalent length, and that each is approximately half the length of the intervening passage; but the 'roughly' and 'approximately' make the foundation too insecure for any conjectural superstructure.[1]

Finally, there are the passages which the Folio omits. These present a comparatively simple problem, since the great majority of them are passages more effective from a poetic than a dramatic standpoint, or in some other way such as would naturally fall under the axe in 'cutting' the play, already very long, for presentation. The portents in Rome disappear (I. i. 108-25), and so do the observations on drunkenness (I. iv. 17-38); the more sententious portions of Hamlet's speeches in III. iv. are cut, and so too are the over-

---

[1] The fact that Q 1 does mention, however briefly, the children, gives some support to the idea that this passage was rather an omission (by carelessness or design) from Q 2 than an insertion in F.

anticipatory lines (202-10) in the same scene. IV. iv. is drastically handled, the whole 'How all occasions' soliloquy disappearing together with the passage introducing it, and nothing being left but a rather unnecessary march of Fortinbras and his army over the stage. IV. vii. gains by the loss of three pieces of unneeded material. A certain amount of Osric disappears from V. ii., and all of 'a Lord,' perhaps because it was felt that the climax was being unduly delayed. The second of the Osric omissions is interesting, since we can see the cutter joining the edges of his cut (see the note on V. ii. 136-40). (It will be noticed that three of these passages, besides being dramatically otiose, are also corrupt, which would be an additional reason for the Folio reviser to deal with them by the easy road of omission.) And when we find that at least some of the Folio additions are of the same type, e.g. the quadruple 'o' after 'the rest is silence,' and the effective exit remark at the end of IV. ii., it is hard to resist the conclusion that a great proportion of the Folio alterations represent alterations made in the playhouse, possibly over a considerable period, as they were found to be effective in presentation. They may or may not have been made by Shakespeare himself; they are at least not beyond the capacity of any reasonably competent adapter. But if we admit the two considerable Folio insertions discussed above as being Shakespeare's own, we must admit at least the possibility that he revised more extensively.

At any rate it is clear from what has been said that the practice of giving as the *textus receptus* of this play the whole of both Quarto and Folio versions is quite uncritical. If the bulk of the Folio alterations are not Shakespeare's own they have no authority, and we need not trouble ourselves about them, except where they help to correct verbal errors; if they are his own we are not entitled to pick and choose; if he added some passages he also omitted many more, and to print all the passages without distinction produces a state of the play which its author certainly never intended. The text here given is something of a compromise. It is based throughout verbally on Q 2. In the interests of readability in a number of places where F appears to make a reasonably certain emendation the Folio reading is accepted, often without comment; but even so, this text remains verbally nearer to Q 2 than most. The great majority of the passages which are not common to both texts are indicated, passages which occur only in Q 2 being enclosed in square brackets [ ], and those which occur only in Folio being enclosed in brace brackets { }. It is hoped that this will make it possible for the reader, without too much distraction, to read either text he chooses, and will also, when supplemented by the notes, give him adequate illustrations of the kind of differences that are observable between the Quarto and Folio texts in general.

The Sources and Development of the Play. The main source of *Hamlet* is a Norse legend which first appears in a history of the Danes by Saxo Grammaticus at the end of the twelfth century. The following is Professor Dowden's summary :—

"Horwendil and his brother Feng rule Jutland under King Rorik of Denmark. Horwendil slays Koll, King of Norway, and marries Gerutha, the daughter of King Rorik ; their son is Amleth. Feng, jealous of his brother, slays Horwendil, and takes Gerutha to wife. Amleth feigns to be dull of wits and little better than a beast, while secretly planning vengeance. He baffles the courtiers by riddling words, which for them are nonsense, but are really significant. A girl, his foster-sister, is placed in his way, in the hope that his conduct may betray his true state of mind ; his foster-brother warns him of the snare, and he baffles his enemies. A friend of Feng, 'more confident than wise,' proposes to act as eavesdropper during an interview between Amleth and his mother. Amleth, crowing like a cock, flapping his arms like wings, and leaping hither and thither, discovers the eavesdropper hidden under straw, stabs him and brutally disposes of the body. He explains to his mother that his madness is feigned and that he plans revenge, and he gains her over to his side. His uncle sends Amleth to Britain, with two companions, who bear a letter graven on wood, requesting the king to slay Amleth. The letter is altered by Amleth, and his companions are put to death. His adventures in Britain do not affect Shakespeare's play. He returns, makes the courtiers drunk, sets them in hangings knitted by his mother, sets fire to the palace, and slays his uncle with the sword. He harangues the people, and is hailed as Feng's successor. After other adventures of crafty device and daring deed, Amleth dies in battle. Had he lived, favoured by nature and fortune, he would have surpassed Hercules." There clearly are the main outlines of the story, whatever differences there are in the character of Hamlet and the manner of his death.

As early as 1589 there was an English *Hamlet* on the stage based presumably upon this story. There are two allusions to it, one in a Preface by Nash to Greene's *Menaphon* :—

" It is a common practise now a daies amongst a sort of shifting companions, that runne through every arte, and thrive by none, to leave the trade of *Noverint*, whereto they were borne, and busie themselves with the indevors of Art, that could scarcelie latinize their necke-verse if they should have neede ; yet English *Seneca* read by candle light yeeldes manie good sentences, as *Bloud is a begger*, and so foorth ; and, if you intreate him faire in a frostie morning, he will afoord you whole *Hamlets*, I should say handfulls of tragical speaches." And another in 1596 by Lodge, when he wrote of one who looked " as pale as the visard of the ghost, which cried so miserably at the theater, like an oyster-wife, *Hamlet revenge*." This *Hamlet* was probably, though not certainly, by Thomas Kyd, and it is again probable, though again not certain, that the first form of Shakespeare's *Hamlet*, imperfectly represented by Q 1, is a re-writing of this play of Kyd's. At all events, all of the development that we can make any attempt to study is the transition from the stage represented by Q 1, whatever we suppose that stage to have been, to Q 2, and so onwards (if we are determined to see Shakespeare's hand in the alterations) to the modified form of F.

Duration of Time. There are difficulties about this, almost all concerned, as is usual with Shakespeare, with the position and length of the intervals. And the difficulties are made worse by the traditional division of acts, which as regards the last three acts has no authority. The First Act is clear enough; it runs from midnight to shortly after the following midnight. There is then an interval of two months. Act II., Act III., and Act IV. i.-iv. inclusive would go into another somewhat crowded twenty-four hours, from, say, noon till noon, if it were not that at the end of II. Hamlet says that they will have the play ' *to-morrow night*,' and at the beginning of III. Rosencrantz and Guildenstern mention the play as being ' *this night*.' [1] We must therefore assume an interval of twenty-four hours between II. and III. After IV. iv. there is another interval while Hamlet is on the seas. IV. v.-vii. take up part of a day. Between IV. vii. and V. i. there appears to be an interval of a night, since the King in the graveyard mentions to Laertes their 'last night's speech.' But none of these difficulties worries the spectator or the reader unless he perversely looks for them.

[1] For this reason the view that Act III. should open with III. ii. appears untenable.

Criticism. There is perhaps no dramatic work in the world which has accumulated round it such a mass of criticism of all kinds. It has been a perpetual challenge to the critics, inspiring them to their most brilliant interpretations, or dragging them down to the depths of fatuity. It has been studied as a great play, which it is, and as a problem in pathological psychology, which at least it was never intended to be. We get nowhere in our appreciation of *Hamlet* if we allow ourselves for one moment to forget that, however wonderful and profound a 'study in human nature' Shakespeare's genius and insight made of it, the play of *Hamlet* is, in its essence, a superb melodrama of revenge, a play for the Elizabethan stage. And I propose to run away from the problem of selecting adequately from the wealth of criticism, good and bad, by giving two passages only. The first is from Johnson, in his coolest mood. "If the dramas of Shakspeare were to be characterised, each by the particular excellence which distinguishes it from the rest, we must allow to the tragedy of *Hamlet* the praise of variety. The incidents are so numerous, that the argument of the play would make a long tale. The scenes are interchangeably diversified with merriment and solemnity; with merriment that includes judicious and instructive observations; and solemnity, not strained by poetical violence above the natural sentiments of man. New characters appear from time to time in continual succession, exhibiting various forms of life and particular modes of conversation. The pretended madness of Hamlet causes much mirth, the mournful distraction of Ophelia fills the heart with tenderness, and every personage produces the effect intended, from the Apparition, that in the First Act chills the blood with horror, to the Fop in the last, that exposes affectation to just contempt. The conduct is perhaps not wholly secure against objections. The action is indeed for the most part in continual progression, but there are some scenes which neither forward nor retard it. Of the feigned madness of Hamlet there appears no adequate cause, for he does nothing which he might not have done with the reputation of sanity. He plays the madman most, when he treats Ophelia with so much rudeness, which seems to be useless and wanton cruelty.

"Hamlet is, through the whole piece, rather an instrument than an agent. After he has, by the stratagem of the play, convicted the King, he makes no attempt to punish him; and his death is at last effected by an incident which Hamlet had no part in producing.

"The catastrophe is not very happily produced; the exchange of weapons is rather an expedient of necessity, than a stroke of art. A scheme might easily be formed to kill Hamlet with the dagger, and Laertes with the bowl.

"The poet is accused of having shown little regard to poetical justice, and may be charged with equal neglect of poetical probability. The apparition left the regions of the dead to little purpose; the revenge which he demands is not obtained but by the death of him that was required to take it; and the gratification, which would arise from the destruction of an usurper and a murderer, is abated by the untimely death of Ophelia, the young, the beautiful, the harmless, and the pious."

The other extract is from a criticism of the play which seems to me, for concision, penetration and balance, as brilliant as one could wish, but which is much less known than it deserves to be, since it is the Introduction to a small, almost a 'school' edition of the play edited in 1912 for the Clarendon Press[1] by Professor G. S. Gordon. It is, amongst other excellent things, an excellent antidote to the Goethe-Coleridge view of *Hamlet*.

[1] By whose permission the following passage is quoted.

HAMLET

" The ordinary view of *Hamlet* comes from Coleridge. It was the opinion of Coleridge, and therefore of the nineteenth century, that the central thing in *Hamlet* is a problem of conduct; that Shakespeare's chief purpose in writing the play was to exhibit a character in which reflection fatally prevailed over the principle of action. This is a false opinion, which time will destroy. What we see in *Hamlet* is not a moral problem, but a tragic situation; not a problem of character, but an experiment of fate; not a problem of conduct, but the agonies of a soul. . . .

" Coleridge's opinion, when it was first expressed, was a novelty in England. Goethe had said something like it in his *Wilhelm Meister*, but Goethe at this time was unknown to most Englishmen except by name. We are asked to suppose, then, that Coleridge was the first English writer who grasped the meaning of a play which had been read and acted with applause since the reign of James. To suppose this would be to lampoon two centuries. . . .

" If Coleridge was the first man in England to understand the play, how did England contrive to enjoy it so thoroughly for two centuries without understanding it? . . .

" I said that *Hamlet* was not so much the study of a temperament as the study of a tragic situation. Let us examine the situation more closely. A son, already shocked by his father's sudden death, disgusted by his mother's second marriage, and irritated at the frustration of his natural ambitions (for he was heir to the crown), is stirred to the depths by a supernatural message from his father, his idol among men. This brings to a head two feelings already in some ferment: disgust at the part of women in the world, and rage at the ineffectiveness of his position and the rusting of his powers. The command of his father is one which he cannot refuse. He would do anything for his father. But the circumstances are such as to bring into question the foundations of life. It is not the mere business of revenge that perplexes him. He is as capable of doing this in a heat as any man. The whole basis of the family is upset, and he must rake among the ruins before he can act. He must think things out. He must be resolved on the question of the use of living at all. Why act, if all action is part of a vain and disgusting show, corrupt from the first institution of men and women, from the first parents? Had his uncle alone been concerned, Hamlet would have behaved very differently. But his mother is concerned also: how much or how little he does not know. It is this, not the call to stab, which 'palsies him o'er.' An active administrative man, you may say, would have collected proofs. But there were none, except the word of a ghost, and no one heard that word but Hamlet. He might, then, have addressed himself to the people, and relying on his greater popularity might have dethroned his uncle and dealt with him as he liked? But it was more than a public matter. It was a family scandal. The honour not only of his house but of humanity was concerned. His mother was in it. These were the 'stimulating circumstances' in which Hamlet was placed. These were the circumstances in which he was obliged to act 'on the spur of the moment.' Why on the spur of the moment? His father, after all, was dead. His mother, after all, was married. The situation was morally past cure, irremediable except by the hand of God, a case for the next world. Why, then, this cry about immediate action? There was not only no need for such action (though Hamlet in his wildness naturally talks as if there were), but no action that could be taken could make things better. There was revenge, of course; and this, I suppose, is what Coleridge describes as 'being called upon to act by every motive human and divine.' Hamlet could satisfy revenge;

but he could no more heal the situation than he could call his father back from the dead or undo his mother's frailty. He could only pile one dead body on another. It is the feeling of this (for Hamlet felt it if we do not) that guides him on his strange sidling progress through the play. Now this feeling is the feeling of Fate.

" It was remarked by Johnson, and it has been repeated by every one since, that Hamlet is throughout the play rather an instrument than an agent. ' After he has, by the stratagem of the play, convicted the King, he makes no attempt to punish him, and his death is at last effected by an incident which Hamlet has no part in producing.' This the critics put down to weakness of Will. They should have put it down to Fate. It is Fate, not Will or the weakness of Will, that is the driving genius of the play, and winds it to its end. And this is clear, for there is not an ' agent ' in the play. Hamlet is not the only ' instrument.' All the persons in this tragedy are instruments, and all, like Hamlet, are instruments of Fate. The tragic cause is never in Hamlet alone, nor in anything so single as an individual will. It is in the dynasty to which he belongs. He is a member of a doomed house. His position, therefore, as the hero of the play is delusive. It suggests, both to us and to him, that his will is free. But his will is not free. There is nobody in the play whose will is free, except Horatio, Fortinbras, and others who stand on the circumference of the action. There is a curse on the family which even the sentinels feel in the first scene, and it swallows them all, murderer, accomplice, revenger, with all their dependents. Hamlet is the hero only that he may suffer and be the last to fall. The Queen is killed through the man who proved her frailty ; he by Hamlet ; Hamlet by the son of the man whom he had killed in passion ; Laertes by the man whom he had planned to kill by treachery; Polonius, Guildenstern, and Rosencrantz, because they were meddlers and crossed the purposes of Fate. The only innocent victim is Ophelia, and yet she was not innocent either in the eyes of Fate. She had one fault. She belonged to a falling house and loved the heir of another. She fell, therefore, with her family, as Hamlet fell with his. This is the tragedy of *Hamlet*, on the lines of life and destiny. This is the tragedy of *Hamlet* as it was understood before the rise of modern philosophy. This is Shakespeare's *Hamlet* and Saxo's. It is grand and primitive, like a tragedy of the elder Greeks. It is something older and finer than the morbid psychology of the critics. It is the *Hamlet* of every uncorrupted playgoer since 1603."

There are the two extracts. But there is one criticism of the play which, since all readers of it tend to become in greater or less degree also its students, one cannot pass over in silence, though it is so close-knit that it does not lend itself to extract, and that is the relevant chapters in what is certainly one of the greatest, and perhaps the greatest, work of Shakespearean criticism in English, A. C. Bradley's *Shakespearean Tragedy*. Even where all is excellent the section on *Hamlet* stands out, because of the balance which the critic manages to maintain in executing a task of peculiar difficulty. He is conducting a subtle and penetrating analysis of character; and yet he never forgets that the character he is analysing is a character in a play. And I should like to say here what I hope to say elsewhere at greater length, in the companion volume to this edition, with regard to Professor Bradley's methods and results. One sometimes hears his criticism dismissed with the comment, ' Bradley finds in Shakespeare what Shakespeare never meant.' If that means that he finds what is not there, it is I think demonstrably untrue ; if it means that he finds point after point which Shakespeare did not insert of set purpose, then I think that it is true, but very far from damaging. No dramatic artist, surely, of Shakespeare's greatness, when he is at work on a play, says to himself, ' Now I must make this character act thus or say this to illustrate some facet of his character.' He has his character in his mind and he knows from his experience that that character will act thus or say that. But that does not debar the interpretative critic from the closest analysis, and it is one of the clearest tests of a dramatist's greatness and the coherence of his characters that they will stand up to this analysis. And the test of the value of this criticism is simply whether it works. When applied to inferior drama it does not work, and is valueless ; the characters crumble under it. When it is applied to Shakespeare's greatest plays, it illuminates the characters in their full and rounded, and often complex, completeness, and forces one to realise yet more deeply the genius of their creator.

THE TRAGEDY OF
HAMLET, PRINCE OF DENMARK

DRAMATIS PERSONÆ

CLAUDIUS, *king of Denmark.*
HAMLET, *son to the late, and nephew to the present king.*
POLONIUS, *lord chamberlain.*
HORATIO, *friend to Hamlet.*
LAERTES, *son to Polonius.*
VOLTIMAND,
CORNELIUS,
ROSENCRANTZ, } *courtiers.*
GUILDENSTERN,
OSRIC,
A Gentleman,
A Priest.
MARCELLUS, } *officers.*
BARNARDO,
FRANCISCO, *a soldier.*
REYNALDO, *servant to Polonius.*
Players.
Two clowns, *grave-diggers.*
FORTINBRAS, *prince of Norway.*
A Captain.
English Ambassadors.

GERTRUDE, *queen of Denmark, and mother to Hamlet.*
OPHELIA, *daughter to Polonius.*

Lords, Ladies, Officers, Soldiers, Sailors, Messengers, and other
Attendants.

Ghost of Hamlet's Father.

SCENE : *Denmark.*

THE TRAGEDY OF
HAMLET, PRINCE OF DENMARK

Act First

SCENE I

Elsinore.   A platform before the castle

Francisco at his post.   Enter to him Barnardo

Bar. Who's there?

Fra. Nay, answer me: stand and unfold yourself.

Bar. Long live the king!

Fra. Barnardo?

Bar. He.

Fra. You come most carefully upon your hour.

Bar. 'Tis now struck twelve; get thee to bed, Francisco.

Fra. For this relief much thanks, 'tis bitter cold,
And I am sick at heart.

Bar. Have you had quiet guard?

Fra.   Not a mouse stirring.   10

Bar. Well, good night.
If you do meet Horatio and Marcellus,
The rivals of my watch, bid them make haste.

Fra. I think I hear them ; Stand ho, who is there ?

Enter Horatio and Marcellus

Hor. Friends to this ground.

Mar. And liegemen to the Dane.

Fra. Give you good night.

Mar. O, farewell, honest soldier,
Who hath reliev'd you ?

Fra. Barnardo hath my place ;
Give you good night. *Exit*

Mar. Holla, Barnardo !

Bar. Say,
What, is Horatio there ?

Hor. A piece of him.

Bar. Welcome Horatio, welcome good Marcellus.   20

Hor. What, has this thing appear'd again to-night ?

Bar. I have seen nothing.

Mar. Horatio says 'tis but our fantasy,
And will not let belief take hold of him,
Touching this dreaded sight twice seen of us ;
Therefore I have entreated him along,
With us to watch the minutes of this night,
That if again this apparition come,
He may approve our eyes and speak to it.

Hor. Tush, tush, 'twill not appear.

Bar. Sit down a while,   30

And let us once again assail your ears,
That are so fortified against our story,
What we have two nights seen.

Hor.   Well, sit we down,
And let us hear Barnardo speak of this.

Bar. Last night of all,
When yond same star that's westward from the pole
Had made his course to illume that part of heaven
Where now it burns, Marcellus and myself,
The bell then beating one,—

Enter Ghost

Mar. Peace, break thee off, look, where it comes again !   40
Bar. In the same figure like the king that's dead.
Mar. Thou art a scholar, speak to it, Horatio.
Bar. Looks it not like the king ? mark it, Horatio.
Hor. Most like ; it horrors me with fear and wonder.
Bar. It would be spoke to.
Mar.   Speak to it, Horatio.
Hor. What art thou that usurp'st this time of night,
Together with that fair and warlike form,
In which the majesty of buried Denmark
Did sometimes march ? by heaven I charge thee speak !
Mar. It is offended.
Bar.   See, it stalks away.   50
Hor. Stay, speak, speak, I charge thee speak !   *Exit Ghost*

3

Mar. 'Tis gone, and will not answer.

Bar. How now, Horatio? you tremble and look pale:
Is not this something more than fantasy?
What think you on 't?

Hor. Before my God I might not this believe,
Without the sensible and true avouch
Of mine own eyes.

Mar. Is it not like the king?

Hor. As thou art to thyself.
Such was the very armour he had on,   60
When he the ambitious Norway combated;
So frown'd he once, when, in an angry parle,
He smote the sleaded pollax on the ice.   †
'Tis strange.

Mar. Thus twice before, and jump at this dead hour,
With martial stalk hath he gone by our watch.

Hor. In what particular thought to work I know not,
But in the gross and scope of my opinion,
This bodes some strange eruption to our state.

Mar. Good now, sit down, and tell me, he that knows,   70
Why this same strict and most observant watch
So nightly toils the subject of the land,
And why such daily cast of brazen cannon,
And foreign mart for implements of war,
Why such impress of shipwrights, whose sore task

Does not divide the Sunday from the week;
What might be toward, that this sweaty haste
Doth make the night joint-labourer with the day:
Who is 't that can inform me?

Hor.   That can I.
At least the whisper goes so; our last king,   80
Whose image even but now appear'd to us,
Was, as you know, by Fortinbras of Norway,
Thereto prick'd on by a most emulate pride,
Dar'd to the combat; in which our valiant Hamlet
(For so this side of our known world esteem'd him)
Did slay this Fortinbras; who by a seal'd compact,
Well ratified by law and heraldry,
Did forfeit, with his life, all those his lands
Which he stood seiz'd of, to the conqueror:
Against the which a moiety competent   90
Was gaged by our king, which had return'd
To the inheritance of Fortinbras,
Had he been vanquisher; as, by the same cov'nant
And carriage of the article design'd,
His fell to Hamlet; now sir, young Fortinbras,
Of unimproved metal, hot and full,
Hath in the skirts of Norway here and there
Shark'd up a list of lawless resolutes,
For food and diet, to some enterprise

C   5

That hath a stomach in't, which is no other　　100
(As it doth well appear unto our state)
But to recover of us by strong hand
And terms compulsatory, those foresaid lands
So by his father lost; and this, I take it,
Is the main motive of our preparations,
The source of this our watch, and the chief head
Of this post-haste and romage in the land.

[*Bar.* I think it be no other, but e'en so;
Well may it sort that this portentous figure
Comes armed through our watch so like the king　　110
That was and is the question of these wars.

Hor. A mote it is to trouble the mind's eye:
In the most high and palmy state of Rome,
A little ere the mightiest Julius fell,
The graves stood tenantless, and the sheeted dead
Did squeak and gibber in the Roman streets:

.　　.　　.　　.　　.　　.

And even the like precurse of fear'd events,
As harbingers preceding still the fates
And prologue to the omen coming on,
Have heaven and earth together demonstrated　　120
Unto our climatures and countrymen.]
As stars with trains of fire, and dews of blood,
Disasters in the sun; and the moist star,

6

Upon whose influence Neptune's empire stands,
Was sick almost to doomsday with eclipse:

Re-enter Ghost

But soft, behold, lo where it comes again !
I 'll cross it though it blast me ; stay, illusion ;
If thou hast any sound or use of voice,
Speak to me,
If there be any good thing to be done   130
That may to thee do ease, and grace to me,
Speak to me,
If thou art privy to thy country's fate,
(Which happily foreknowing may avoid)
O, speak !
Or if thou hast uphoarded in thy life
Extorted treasure in the womb of earth,
For which, they say, your spirits oft walk in death,
Speak of it, stay and speak ! (*The cock crows.*) Stop it,
Marcellus.

Mar. Shall I strike it with my partisan ?   140
Hor. Do, if it will not stand.
Bar.   'Tis here !
Hor.   'Tis here !
Mar. 'Tis gone !   *Exit Ghost*
We do it wrong, being so majestical,
To offer it the show of violence ;

7

For it is as the air, invulnerable,
And our vain blows malicious mockery.

Bar. It was about to speak when the cock crew.

Hor. And then it started like a guilty thing,
Upon a fearful summons ; I have heard,
The cock that is the trumpet to the morn   150
Doth with his lofty and shrill-sounding throat
Awake the god of day, and at his warning,
Whether in sea or fire, in earth or air,
The extravagant and erring spirit hies
To his confine ; and of the truth herein
This present object made probation.

Mar. It faded on the crowing of the cock.
Some say that ever 'gainst that season comes
Wherein our Saviour's birth is celebrated,
The bird of dawning singeth all night long,   160
And then they say no spirit dare stir abroad,
The nights are wholesome, then no planets strike,
No fairy takes, nor witch hath power to charm,
So hallow'd, and so gracious is that time.

Hor. So have I heard and do in part believe it.
But look, the morn in russet mantle clad
Walks o'er the dew of yon high eastward hill :
Break we our watch up ; and by my advice
Let us impart what we have seen to-night

Unto young Hamlet, for upon my life   170
This spirit, dumb to us, will speak to him :
Do you consent we shall acquaint him with it,
As needful in our loves, fitting our duty ?

*Mar.*Let 's do 't, I pray ; and I this morning know
Where we shall find him most convenient.

Exeunt

to L throne

U.R.

SCENE II

A room of state in the castle

Flourish. Enter the King, Queen, Polonius, Laertes,
Voltimand, Cornelius, Lords, Attendants ; and Hamlet.

Ki. Though yet of Hamlet our dear brother's death
The memory be green, and that it us befitted
To bear our hearts in grief, and our whole kingdom
To be contracted in one brow of woe.
Yet so far hath discretion fought with nature
That we with wisest sorrow think on him
Together with remembrance of ourselves :
Therefore our sometime sister, now our queen,
The imperial jointress to this warlike state,
Have we, as 'twere with a defeated joy,   10
With an auspicious and a dropping eye,

9

With mirth in funeral, and with dirge in marriage,
In equal scale weighing delight and dole,
Taken to wife : nor have we herein barr'd
Your better wisdoms, which have freely gone
With this affair along.   For all, our thanks.
Now follows that you know; young Fortinbras,
Holding a weak supposal of our worth,
Or thinking by our late dear brother's death
Our state to be disjoint, and out of frame,   20
Colleagued with this dream of his advantage,
He hath not fail'd to pester us with message
Importing the surrender of those lands
Lost by his father, with all bands of law,
To our most valiant brother ; so much for him.
Now for ourself, and for this time of meeting,
Thus much the business is ; we have here writ
To Norway, uncle of young Fortinbras,
Who, impotent and bed-rid, scarcely hears
Of this his nephew's purpose, to suppress   30
His further gait herein, in that the levies,
The lists and full proportions, are all made
Out of his subject ; and we here dispatch
You good Cornelius, and you Voltimand,
For bearers of this greeting to old Norway,
Giving to you no further personal power

To business with the king, more than the scope
Of these delated articles allow :
Farewell, and let your haste commend your duty.

Cor. ⎫
Vol. ⎭ In that and all things will we show our duty.   40

Ki. We doubt it nothing, heartily farewell.

                              Exeunt Voltimand and Cornelius

And now, Laertes, what 's the news with you ?
You told us of some suit, what is 't, Laertes ?
You cannot speak of reason to the Dane
And lose your voice : what wouldst thou beg, Laertes,
That shall not be my offer, not thy asking ?
The head is not more native to the heart,
The hand more instrumental to the mouth,
Than is the throne of Denmark to thy father.
What wouldst thou have, Laertes ?

Lae.   My dread lord,   50
Your leave and favour to return to France,
From whence, though willingly I came to Denmark,
To show my duty in your coronation,
Yet now, I must confess, that duty done,
My thoughts and wishes bend again toward France
And bow them to your gracious leave and pardon.

Ki. Have you your father's leave ?   What says Polonius ?

Pol. He hath, my lord, [wrung from me my slow leave

By laboursome petition, and at last
Upon his will I seal'd my hard consent :]   60
I do beseech you give him leave to go.
Ki. Take thy fair hour, Laertes ; time be thine,
And thy best graces spend it at thy will !
But now, my cousin Hamlet, and my son,—
Ham. (*aside*) A little more than kin, and less than kind.   †
Ki. How is it that the clouds still hang on you ?
Ham. Not so [much], my lord ; I am too much in the sun.
Qu. Good Hamlet, cast thy nighted colour off,
And let thine eye look like a friend on Denmark ;
Do not for ever with thy vailed lids   70
Seek for thy noble father in the dust ;
Thou know'st 'tis common, all that lives must die,
Passing through nature to eternity.
Ham. Ay, madam, it is common.
Qu.   If it be,
Why seems it so particular with thee ?
Ham. ' Seems,' madam ? nay, it is, I know not ' seems.'
'Tis not alone my inky cloak, good mother,
Nor customary suits of solemn black,
Nor windy suspiration of forc'd breath,
No, nor the fruitful river in the eye,   80
Nor the dejected haviour of the visage,
Together with all forms, moods, shapes of grief,

That can denote me truly ; these indeed seem,
For they are actions that a man might play,
But I have that within which passes show,
These but the trappings and the suits of woe.

Ki. 'Tis sweet and commendable in your nature, Hamlet,
To give these mourning duties to your father :
But you must know your father lost a father,
That father lost, lost his, and the survivor bound   90
In filial obligation for some term
To do obsequious sorrow ; but to persever
In obstinate condolement is a course
Of impious stubbornness, 'tis unmanly grief,
It shows a will most incorrect to heaven,
A heart unfortified, a mind impatient,
An understanding simple and unschool'd :
For what we know must be and is as common
As any the most vulgar thing to sense,
Why should we in our peevish opposition   100
Take it to heart ?   Fie ! 'tis a fault to heaven,
A fault against the dead, a fault to nature,
To reason most absurd, whose common theme
Is death of fathers, and who still hath cried,
From the first corse, till he that died to-day,
' This must be so.'   We pray you throw to earth
This unprevailing woe, and think of us

As of a father : for let the world take note,
You are the most immediate to our throne,
And with no less nobility of love   110
Than that which dearest father bears his son
Do I impart toward you.   For your intent
In going back to school in Wittenberg,
It is most retrograde to our desire,
And we beseech you, bend you to remain
Here in the cheer and comfort of our eye,
Our chiefest courtier, cousin, and our son.

Qu. Let not thy mother lose her prayers, Hamlet :
I pray thee, stay with us ; go not to Wittenberg.

Ham. I shall in all my best obey you, madam.   120

Ki. Why, 'tis a loving and a fair reply :
Be as ourself in Denmark.   Madam, come ;
This gentle and unforc'd accord of Hamlet
Sits smiling to my heart, in grace whereof,
No jocund health that Denmark drinks to-day,
But the great cannon to the clouds shall tell,
And the king's rouse the heaven shall bruit again,
Re-speaking earthly thunder.   Come away.

      Flourish.   Exeunt all but Hamlet

Ham. O that this too too sullied flesh would melt,
Thaw and resolve itself into a dew,   130
Or that the Everlasting had not fix'd

His canon 'gainst self-slaughter !   O God, O God,
How weary, stale, flat, and unprofitable
Seem to me all the uses of this world !
Fie on 't, ah fie ! 'tis an unweeded garden
That grows to seed ; things rank and gross in nature
Possess it merely.   That it should come to this !
But two months dead, nay, not so much, not two ;
So excellent a king, that was to this
Hyperion to a satyr, so loving to my mother,   140
That he might not beteem the winds of heaven
Visit her face too roughly ; heaven and earth,
Must I remember ? why, she should hang on him,
As if increase of appetite had grown
By what it fed on, and yet within a month—
Let me not think on 't ; frailty, thy name is woman !
A little month, or ere those shoes were old
With which she follow'd my poor father's body,
Like Niobe, all tears :—why she, {even she,—}
O God, a beast that wants discourse of reason   150
Would have mourn'd longer,—married with my uncle,
My father's brother, but no more like my father
Than I to Hercules : within a month,
Ere yet the salt of most unrighteous tears
Had left the flushing in her galled eyes,
She married ; O most wicked speed, to post

15

With such dexterity to incestuous sheets !
It is not, nor it cannot come to good ;
But break my heart, for I must hold my tongue !
   Enter Horatio, Marcellus, and Barnardo

Hor. Hail to your lordship !
Ham.   I am glad to see you well : 160
  Horatio, or I do forget myself.
Hor. The same, my lord, and your poor servant ever.
Ham. Sir, my good friend ; I 'll change that name with †
  you ;
  And what make you from Wittenberg, Horatio ?
  Marcellus.
Mar. My good lord.
Ham. I am very glad to see you. (*to Bar.*) Good even, sir.
  (*to Hor.*) But what, in faith, make you from Wittenberg ?
Hor. A truant disposition, good my lord.
Ham. I would not hear your enemy say so, 170
  Nor shall you do my ear that violence
  To make it truster of your own report
  Against yourself : I know you are no truant :
  But what is your affair in Elsinore ?
  We 'll teach you for to drink ere you depart.
Hor. My lord, I came to see your father's funeral.
Ham. I prithee, do not mock me, fellow-student ;
  I think it was to see my mother's wedding.

Hor. Indeed, my lord, it follow'd hard upon.

Ham. Thrift, thrift, Horatio ; the funeral bak'd-meats 180
    Did coldly furnish forth the marriage tables.
    Would I had met my dearest foe in heaven
    Or ever I had seen that day, Horatio !
    My father, methinks I see my father.

Hor. Where, my lord ?

Ham.   In my mind's eye, Horatio.

Hor. I saw him once ; he was a goodly king.

Ham. He was a man, take him for all in all,
    I shall not look upon his like again.

Hor. My lord, I think I saw him yesternight.

Ham. Saw ? who ? 190

Hor. My lord, the king your father.

Ham.   The king my father ?

Hor. Season your admiration for a while
    With an attent ear, till I may deliver,
    Upon the witness of these gentlemen,
    This marvel to you.

Ham.   For God's love, let me hear.

Hor. Two nights together had these gentlemen,
    Marcellus and Barnardo, on their watch,
    In the dead waste and middle of the night,
    Been thus encounter'd.   A figure like your father,
    Armed at point, exactly cap-a-pe, 200

Appears before them, and with solemn march
Goes slow and stately by them : thrice he walk'd
By their oppress'd and fear-surprised eyes,
Within his truncheon's length ; whilst they distill'd
Almost to jelly, with the act of fear
Stand dumb, and speak not to him.   This to me
In dreadful secrecy impart they did,
And I with them the third night kept the watch :
Where, as they had deliver'd, both in time,
Form of the thing, each word made true and good,   210
The apparition comes : I knew your father,
These hands are not more like.

Ham.   But where was this ?

Mar. My lord, upon the platform where we watch.

Ham. Did you not speak to it ?

Hor.   My lord, I did.
But answer made it none ; yet once methought
It lifted up it head and did address
Itself to motion, like as it would speak :
But even then the morning cock crew loud,
And at the sound it shrunk in haste away
And vanish'd from our sight.

Ham.   'Tis very strange.   220

Hor. As I do live my honour'd lord 'tis true,
And we did think it writ down in our duty

To let you know of it.

Ham. Indeed, {indeed,} sirs, but this troubles me.

Hold you the watch to-night ?

Mar.⎤
Bar.⎦　　　　　　　　　　We do, my lord.

Ham. Arm'd, say you ?

Mar.⎤
Bar.⎦　　　　　　　Arm'd, my lord.

Ham.　　　　　　　　　　　From top to toe ?

Mar.⎤
Bar.⎦My lord, from head to foot.

Ham. Then saw you not his face.　　　　　　　　†

Hor. O yes, my lord ; he wore his beaver up.

Ham. What look'd he, frowningly ?　　　　　　230

Hor. A countenance more in sorrow than in anger.

Ham. Pale, or red ?

Hor. Nay, very pale.

Ham.　　　　　　And fix'd his eyes upon you ?

Hor. Most constantly.

Ham.　　　　　　I would I had been there.

Hor. It would have much amaz'd you.

Ham. Very like, {very like.}　Stay'd it long ?

Hor. While one with moderate haste might tell a hundred.

Mar.⎤
Bar.⎦Longer, longer.

19

Hor. Not when I saw 't.

Ham.   His beard was grizzled, no?

Hor. It was as I have seen it in his life,   240
    A sable silver'd.

Ham.   I will watch to-night;
    Perchance 'twill walk again.

Hor.   I warrant it will.

Ham. If it assume my noble father's person,
    I'll speak to it, though hell itself should gape
    And bid me hold my peace; I pray you all,
    If you have hitherto conceal'd this sight,
    Let it be tenable in your silence still,
    And whatsoever else shall hap to-night,
    Give it an understanding, but no tongue:
    I will requite your loves; so fare you well: 250
    Upon the platform, 'twixt eleven and twelve,
    I'll visit you.

All.   Our duty to your honour.

Ham. Your loves, as mine to you: farewell.

                        Exeunt all but Hamlet

    My father's spirit——in arms? all is not well;
    I doubt some foul play; would the night were come!
    Till then sit still, my soul: foul deeds will rise,
    Though all the earth o'erwhelm them to men's eyes.

                                        Exit

SCENE III

A room in Polonius' house

Enter Laertes and Ophelia

Lae. My necessaries are embark'd: farewell:
   And, sister, as the winds give benefit
   And convoy is assistant, do not sleep,
   But let me hear from you.

Oph.   Do you doubt that?

Lae. For Hamlet, and the trifling of his favour,
   Hold it a fashion, and a toy in blood,
   A violet in the youth of primy nature,
   Forward, not permanent, sweet, not lasting,
   The [perfume and] suppliance of a minute;
   No more.

Oph.   No more but so?

Lae.   Think it no more: 10
   For nature crescent does not grow alone
   In thews and bulks, but, as this temple waxes,
   The inward service of the mind and soul
   Grows wide withal; perhaps he loves you now,
   And now no soil nor cautel doth besmirch
   The virtue of his will: but you must fear,
   His greatness weigh'd, his will is not his own;

{For he himself is subject to his birth:} †
He may not, as unvalued persons do,
Carve for himself, for on his choice depends 20
The safety and health of this whole state, †
And therefore must his choice be circumscrib'd
Unto the voice and yielding of that body
Whereof he is the head. Then if he says he loves you,
It fits your wisdom so far to believe it
As he in his particular act and place
May give his saying deed, which is no further
Than the main voice of Denmark goes withal.
Then weigh what loss your honour may sustain,
If with too credent ear you list his songs, 30
Or lose your heart, or your chaste treasure open
To his unmaster'd importunity.
Fear it, Ophelia, fear it, my dear sister,
And keep you in the rear of your affection,
Out of the shot and danger of desire.
The chariest maid is prodigal enough,
If she unmask her beauty to the moon:
Virtue itself 'scapes not calumnious strokes:
The canker galls the infants of the spring
Too oft before their buttons be disclos'd, 40
And in the morn and liquid dew of youth
Contagious blastments are most imminent.

Be wary then ; best safety lies in fear :
Youth to itself rebels, though none else near.

Oph. I shall the effect of this good lesson keep
As watchman to my heart ; but, good my brother,
Do not as some ungracious pastors do,
Show me the steep and thorny way to heaven,
Whiles a puff'd and reckless libertine,
Himself the primrose path of dalliance treads,　　　50
And recks not his own rede.

Lae.　　　　　　　　　　O, fear me not ;
I stay too long : but here my father comes ;
Enter Polonius
A double blessing is a double grace,
Occasion smiles upon a second leave.

Pol. Yet here, Laertes ?　Aboard, aboard, for shame !
The wind sits in the shoulder of your sail,
And you are stay'd for.　There, my blessing with thee,
And these few precepts in thy memory
Look thou character.　Give thy thoughts no tongue,
Nor any unproportion'd thought his act ;　　　60
Be thou familiar, but by no means vulgar ;
Those friends thou hast, and their adoption tried,
Grapple them unto thy soul with hoops of steel,
But do not dull thy palm with entertainment
Of each new-hatch'd unfledg'd comrade ; beware　　†

23

Of entrance to a quarrel, but being in,
Bear 't that the opposed may beware of thee;
Give every man thy ear, but few thy voice;
Take each man's censure, but reserve thy judgement;
Costly thy habit as thy purse can buy, 70
But not express'd in fancy; rich, not gaudy,
For the apparel oft proclaims the man,
And they in France of the best rank and station †
Are of a most select and generous chief in that.
Neither a borrower nor a lender be,
For loan oft loses both itself and friend,
And borrowing dulleth edge of husbandry;
This above all, to thine own self be true,
And it must follow, as the night the day,
Thou canst not then be false to any man. 80
Farewell; my blessing season this in thee!

Lae. Most humbly do I take my leave, my lord.

Pol. The time invites you; go, your servants tend. †

Lae. Farewell, Ophelia, and remember well
What I have said to you.

Oph. 'Tis in my memory lock'd,
And you yourself shall keep the key of it.

Lae. Farewell. *Exit*

Pol. What is 't, Ophelia, he hath said to you?

Oph. So please you, something touching the Lord Hamlet.

24

Pol. Marry, well bethought :   90
    'Tis told me he hath very oft of late
    Given private time to you, and you yourself
    Have of your audience been most free and bounteous :
    If it be so, as so 'tis put on me,
    And that in way of caution, I must tell you,
    You do not understand yourself so clearly
    As it behoves my daughter, and your honour ;
    What is between you ? give me up the truth.

Oph. He hath, my lord, of late made many tenders
    Of his affection to me.   100

Pol. Affection ! pooh ! you speak like a green girl,
    Unsifted in such perilous circumstance ;
    Do you believe his tenders, as you call them ?

Oph. I do not know, my lord, what I should think.

Pol. Marry, I will teach you : think yourself a baby,
    That you have ta'en these tenders for true pay,
    Which are not sterling ; tender yourself more dearly,
    Or (not to crack the wind of the poor phrase,
    Running it thus) you 'll tender me a fool.

Oph. My lord, he hath importun'd me with love   110
    In honourable fashion.

Pol. Ay, fashion you may call it ; go to, go to.

Oph. And hath given countenance to his speech, my lord,
    With [almost] all the [holy] vows of heaven.

Pol. Ay, springes to catch woodcocks. I do know,
When the blood burns, how prodigal the soul
Lends the tongue vows : these blazes, daughter,
Giving more light than heat, extinct in both
Even in their promise, as it is a-making,
You must not take for fire ; from this time   120
Be something scanter of your maiden presence,
Set your entreatments at a higher rate
Than a command to parley ; for Lord Hamlet,
Believe so much in him, that he is young,
And with a larger tether may he walk
Than may be given you : in few, Ophelia,
Do not believe his vows, for they are brokers,
Not of that dye which their investments show,
But mere implorators of unholy suits,
Breathing like sanctified and pious bawds,   130
The better to beguile. This is for all ;
I would not, in plain terms, from this time forth,
Have you so slander any moment leisure,
As to give words or talk with the Lord Hamlet.
Look to 't, I charge you : come your ways.

Oph. I shall obey, my lord.

Exeunt

R

26

SCENE IV

The platform

Enter Hamlet, Horatio, and Marcellus

Ham. The air bites shrewdly; it is very cold.

Hor. It is a nipping and an eager air.

Ham. What hour now?

Hor.   I think it lacks of twelve.

Mar. No, it is struck.

Hor. Indeed? I heard it not: it then draws near the season
    Wherein the spirit held his wont to walk.

            A flourish of trumpets, and two pieces go off
    What does this mean, my lord?

Ham. The king doth wake to-night and takes his rouse,
    Keeps wassail, and the swaggering up-spring reels;
    And as he drains his draughts of Rhenish down,   10
    The kettle-drum and trumpet thus bray out
    The triumph of his pledge.

Hor.   Is it a custom?

Ham. Ay, marry, is 't,
    But to my mind, though I am native here
    And to the manner born, it is a custom
    More honour'd in the breach than the observance.
    [This heavy-headed revel east and west

27

Makes us traduc'd, and tax'd of other nations;
They clepe us drunkards, and with swinish phrase
Soil our addition; and indeed it takes   20
From our achievements, though perform'd at height,
The pith and marrow of our attribute.
So, oft it chances in particular men,
That for some vicious mole of nature in them,
As in their birth, wherein they are not guilty,
(Since nature cannot choose his origin)
By their o'ergrowth of some complexion
Oft breaking down the pales and forts of reason,
Or by some habit, that too much o'er-leavens
The form of plausive manners, that these men,   30
Carrying, I say, the stamp of one defect,
Being nature's livery, or fortune's star,
His virtues else be they as pure as grace,
As infinite as man may undergo,
Shall in the general censure take corruption
From that particular fault: the dram of eale   †
Doth all the noble substance of a doubt
To his own scandal.]

Enter Ghost

Hor.   Look, my lord, it comes!
Ham. Angels and ministers of grace defend us!
Be thou a spirit of health, or goblin damn'd,   40

Bring with thee airs from heaven, or blasts from hell,
Be thy intents wicked, or charitable,
Thou com'st in such a questionable shape,
That I will speak to thee, I'll call thee Hamlet,
King, father, royal Dane: O, answer me,
Let me not burst in ignorance, but tell
Why thy canoniz'd bones, hearsed in death,
Have burst their cerements? why the sepulchre,
Wherein we saw thee quietly interr'd,
Hath op'd his ponderous and marble jaws,   50
To cast thee up again?   What may this mean,
That thou, dead corse, again in complete steel,
Revisits thus the glimpses of the moon,
Making night hideous, and we fools of nature
So horridly to shake our disposition
With thoughts beyond the reaches of our souls?
Say, why is this, wherefore, what should we do?

                                        Ghost beckons

Hor. It beckons you to go away with it,
    As if it some impartment did desire
    To you alone.

Mar.   Look with what courteous action   60
    It waves you to a more removed ground:
    But do not go with it.

Hor.   No, by no means.

                    29

Ham. It will not speak; then I will follow it.

Hor. Do not, my lord.

Ham.   Why, what should be the fear?
I do not set my life at a pin's fee,
And for my soul, what can it do to that,
Being a thing immortal as itself?
It waves me forth again, I'll follow it.

Hor. What if it tempt you toward the flood, my lord,
Or to the dreadful summit of the cliff   70
That bettles o'er his base into the sea,   †
And there assume some other horrible form
Which might deprive your sovereignty of reason,
And draw you into madness? think of it:
[The very place puts toys of desperation,
Without more motive, into every brain
That looks so many fathoms to the sea
And hears it roar beneath.]

Ham.   It waves me still;
Go on, I'll follow thee.

Mar. You shall not go, my lord.

Ham.   Hold off your hands.   80

Hor. Be rul'd, you shall not go.

Ham.   My fate cries out,
And makes each petty arture in this body   †
As hardy as the Nemean lion's nerve.

Still am I call'd; unhand me gentlemen,
By heaven I'll make a ghost of him that lets me:
I say away, go on, I'll follow thee.

>   *Exeunt Ghost and Hamlet*

Hor. He waxes desperate with imagination.

Mar. Let's follow, 'tis not fit thus to obey him.

Hor. Have after, to what issue will this come?

Mar. Something is rotten in the state of Denmark.   90

Hor. Heaven will direct it.

Mar.   Nay, let's follow him.

>   *Exeunt*

SCENE V

Another part of the platform

Enter Ghost and Hamlet

Ham. Whither wilt thou lead me? speak; I'll go no
further.

Gho. Mark me.

Ham.   I will.

Gho.   My hour is almost come
When I to sulph'rous and tormenting flames
Must render up myself.

Ham.   Alas, poor ghost!

31

Gho. Pity me not, but lend thy serious hearing
    To what I shall unfold.

Ham.   Speak ; I am bound to hear.

Gho. So art thou to revenge, when thou shalt hear.

Ham. What ?

Gho. I am thy father's spirit,
    Doom'd for a certain term to walk the night,   10
    And for the day confin'd to fast in fires,
    Till the foul crimes done in my days of nature
    Are burnt and purg'd away : but that I am forbid
    To tell the secrets of my prison-house,
    I could a tale unfold whose lightest word
    Would harrow up thy soul, freeze thy young blood,
    Make thy two eyes like stars start from their spheres,
    Thy knotted and combined locks to part,
    And each particular hair to stand an end,
    Like quills upon the fretful porpentine :   20
    But this eternal blazon must not be
    To ears of flesh and blood.   List, list, O, list !
    If thou didst ever thy dear father love—

Ham. O God !

Gho. Revenge his foul and most unnatural murder.

Ham. Murder ?

Gho. Murder most foul, as in the best it is,
    But this most foul, strange and unnatural.

Ham. Haste me to know 't, that I, with wings as swift
    As meditation, or the thoughts of love,   30
    May sweep to my revenge.

Gho.   I find thee apt,
    And duller shouldst thou be than the fat weed
    That roots itself in ease on Lethe wharf,
    Wouldst thou not stir in this.   Now, Hamlet, hear :
    'Tis given out, that sleeping in my orchard
    A serpent stung me ; so the whole ear of Denmark
    Is by a forged process of my death
    Rankly abus'd : but know, thou noble youth,
    The serpent that did sting thy father's life
    Now wears his crown.

Ham.   O my prophetic soul !   40
    My uncle ?

Gho. Ay, that incestuous, that adulterate beast,
    With witchcraft of his wit, with traitorous gifts,—
    O wicked wit, and gifts that have the power
    So to seduce !—won to his shameful lust
    The will of my most seeming-virtuous queen :
    O Hamlet, what a falling-off was there
    From me, whose love was of that dignity
    That it went hand in hand even with the vow
    I made to her in marriage, and to decline   50
    Upon a wretch whose natural gifts were poor

To those of mine ;
But virtue, as it never will be mov'd,
Though lewdness court it in a shape of heaven.
So lust, though to a radiant angel link'd,
Will sate itself in a celestial bed
And prey on garbage.
But soft ! methinks I scent the morning air,
Brief let me be ; sleeping within my orchard,
My custom always of the afternoon,   60
Upon my secure hour thy uncle stole
With juice of cursed hebona in a vial,
And in the porches of my ears did pour
The leperous distilment, whose effect
Holds such an enmity with blood of man,
That swift as quicksilver it courses through
The natural gates and alleys of the body,
And with a sudden vigour it doth possess   †
And curd, like eager droppings into milk,
The thin and wholesome blood : so did it mine,   70
And a most instant tetter bark'd about,
Most lazar-like, with vile and loathsome crust,
All my smooth body.
Thus was I sleeping by a brother's hand
Of life, of crown, of queen, at once dispatch'd,
Cut off even in the blossoms of my sin,

Unhousel'd, disappointed, unannel'd,
No reckoning made, but sent to my account
With all my imperfections on my head :
O, horrible ! O, horrible ! most horrible !   80
If thou hast nature in thee, bear it not,
Let not the royal bed of Denmark be
A couch for luxury and damned incest.
But, howsoever thou pursues this act,
Taint not thy mind, nor let thy soul contrive
Against thy mother aught ; leave her to heaven,
And to those thorns that in her bosom lodge
To prick and sting her.   Fare thee well at once !
The glow-worm shows the matin to be near,
And 'gins to pale his uneffectual fire :   90
Adieu, adieu, adieu ! remember me.   *Exit*

Ham. O all you host of heaven ! O earth ! what else ?
   And shall I couple hell ?   O, fie !   Hold, [hold,] my
      heart,
   And you, my sinews, grow not instant old,
   But bear me stiffly up.   Remember thee ?
   Ay, thou poor ghost, whiles memory holds a seat
   In this distracted globe.   Remember thee?
   Yea, from the table of my memory
   I'll wipe away all trivial fond records,
   All saws of books, all forms, all pressures past   100

35

That youth and observation copied there,
And thy commandment all alone shall live
Within the book and volume of my brain,
Unmix'd with baser matter : yes, by heaven !
O most pernicious woman !
O villain, villain, smiling, damned villain,
My tables, {my tables,}—meet it is I set it down
That one may smile, and smile, and be a villain,
At least I am sure it may be so in Denmark.   *Writing*
So, uncle, there you are ; now to my word ;   110
It is ' Adieu, adieu ! remember me.'
I have sworn 't.

Hor. (*within*) My lord, my lord !

Mar. (*within*)   Lord Hamlet !

Hor. (*within*)   Heavens secure him !

Ham. So be it !

Mar. Illo, ho, ho, my lord !

Ham. Hillo, ho, ho, boy ! come, bird, come.

Enter Horatio and Marcellus

Mar. How is 't, my noble lord ?

Hor.   What news, my lord ?

Ham. O, wonderful !

Hor. Good my lord, tell it.

Ham.   No, you will reveal it.

Hor. Not I, my lord, by heaven.

Mar.   Nor I, my lord.

Ham. How say you, then ; would heart of man once
      think it ?
    But you 'll be secret ?

Hor. ⎫
Mar. ⎭   Ay, by heaven, {my lord.}

Ham. There 's never a villain dwelling in all Denmark
    But he 's an arrant knave.

Hor. There needs no ghost, my lord, come from the grave
    To tell us this.

Ham.   Why, right, you are in the right,
    And so, without more circumstance at all,
    I hold it fit that we shake hands and part,
    You, as your business and desire shall point you,
    For every man hath business and desire,   130
    Such as it is, and for my own poor part,
    I will go pray.

Hor. These are but wild and whirling words, my lord.

Ham. I am sorry they offend you, heartily;
    Yes, faith, heartily.

Hor.   There 's no offence, my lord.

Ham. Yes, by Saint Patrick, but there is, Horatio,   †
    And much offence too; touching this vision here,
    It is an honest ghost, that let me tell you:
    For your desire to know what is between us,

E

O'ermaster 't as you may ; and now, good friends,   140
As you are friends, scholars, and soldiers,
Give me one poor request.

Hor. What is 't, my lord ? we will.

Ham. Never make known what you have seen to-night.

Hor.
Mar. } My lord, we will not.

Ham.   Nay, but swear 't.

Hor.   In faith,
My lord, not I.

Mar.   Nor I, my lord, in faith.

Ham. Upon my sword.

Mar.   We have sworn, my lord, already.

Ham. Indeed, upon my sword, indeed.

                        Ghost cries under the stage

Gho. Swear.

Ham. Ha, ha, boy, say'st thou so ? art thou there, true-
            penny ?   150
Come on, you hear this fellow in the cellarage ;
Consent to swear.

Hor.   Propose the oath, my lord.

Ham. Never to speak of this that you have seen,
Swear by my sword.

Gho. Swear.

Ham. *Hic, et ubique ?* then we 'll shift our ground.

38

Come hither, gentlemen,
And lay your hands again upon my sword:
Swear by my sword,
Never to speak of this that you have heard.   160

Gho. Swear by his sword.

Ham. Well said, old mole! canst work i' the earth so fast?
A worthy pioner! Once more remove, good friends.

Hor. O day and night, but this is wondrous strange!

Ham. And therefore as a stranger give it welcome;
There are more things in heaven and earth, Horatio,
Than are dreamt of in your philosophy; but come,
Here, as before, never, so help you mercy,
(How strange or odd some'er I bear myself,
As I perchance hereafter shall think meet   170
To put an antic disposition on)
That you, at such times seeing me, never shall,
With arms encumber'd thus, or this head-shake,   †
Or by pronouncing of some doubtful phrase,
(As 'Well, well, we know,' or 'We could, an if we
        would,'
Or 'If we list to speak,' or 'There be, an if they
        might,'
Or such ambiguous giving out) to note
That you know aught of me: this do swear,   †
So grace and mercy at your most need help you.

Gho. Swear.

Ham. Rest, rest, perturbed spirit   (*They swear.*) So, gentlemen,
 With all my love I do commend me to you,
 And what so poor a man as Hamlet is
 May do t' express his love and friending to you,
 God willing, shall not lack : let us go in together,
 And still your fingers on your lips, I pray.
 The time is out of joint ; O cursed spite,
 That ever I was born to set it right !
 Nay, come, let 's go together.   *Exeunt*

Act Second

SCENE I

Two months later

A room in Polonius' house

Enter Polonius and Reynaldo

Pol. Give him this money, and these notes, Reynaldo.
Rey. I will, my lord.
Pol. You shall do marvellous wisely, good Reynaldo,
 Before you visit him, to make inquire

40

Of his behaviour.

Rey.   My lord, I did intend it.

Pol. Marry, well said, very well said.   Look you, sir,
Inquire me first what Danskers are in Paris,
And how, and who, what means, and where they keep,
What company, at what expense, and finding
By this encompassment and drift of question   10
That they do know my son, come you more nearer
Than your particular demands will touch it :
Take you, as 'twere, some distant knowledge of him,
As thus, ' I know his father, and his friends,
And in part him : ' do you mark this, Reynaldo ?

Rey. Ay, very well, my lord.

Pol. ' And in part him ; but,' you may say, ' not well :
But if 't be he I mean, he 's very wild,
Addicted so and so ; ' and there put on him
What forgeries you please ; marry, none so rank   20
As may dishonour him, take heed of that,
But, sir, such wanton, wild, and usual slips
As are companions noted and most known
To youth and liberty.

Rey.   As gaming, my lord.

Pol. Ay, or drinking, fencing, swearing,
Quarrelling, drabbing : you may go so far.

Rey. My lord, that would dishonour him.

Pol. Faith, no, as you may season it in the charge,
You must not put another scandal on him,
That he is open to incontinency,   30
That's not my meaning, but breathe his faults so
    quaintly
That they may seem the taints of liberty,
The flash and outbreak of a fiery mind,
A savageness in unreclaimed blood,
Of general assault.

Rey.   But, my good lord,—

Pol. Wherefore should you do this?

Rey.   Ay, my lord,
I would know that.

Pol.   Marry, sir, here's my drift,
And I believe it is a fetch of warrant:
You laying these slight sullies on my son,
As 'twere a thing a little soil'd with working,   40
Mark you,
Your party in converse, him you would sound,
Having ever seen in the prenominate crimes
The youth you breathe of guilty, be assur'd
He closes with you in this consequence;
'Good sir,' (or so) or 'friend,' or 'gentleman,'
According to the phrase or the addition
Of man and country.

42

Rey.   Very good, my lord.

Pol. And then, sir, does he this—he does—what was I
about to say? By the mass, I was about to say   50
something: where did I leave?

Rey. At 'closes in the consequence,' {at 'friend or so,'
and ' gentleman.'}   †

Pol. At 'closes in the consequence,' ay, marry;
He closes {with you} thus: ' I know the gentleman;
I saw him yesterday, or t' other day,
Or then, or then, with such, or such, and, as you say,
There was a' gaming, there o'ertook in 's rouse,
There falling out at tennis: ' or perchance,
' I saw him enter such a house of sale,'   60
Videlicet, a brothel, or so forth.   See you now,
Your bait of falsehood takes this carp of truth:
And thus do we of wisdom and of reach,
With windlasses and with assays of bias,
By indirections find directions out:
So, by my former lecture and advice,
Shall you my son.   You have me, have you not?

Rey. My lord, I have.

Pol.   God be wi' ye; fare ye well.

Rey. Good my lord!

Pol. Observe his inclination in yourself.   70

Rey. I shall, my lord.

Pol. And let him ply his music.

Rey.   Well, my lord.

Pol. Farewell !   *Exit Reynaldo*

Enter Ophelia

How now, Ophelia ! what's the matter ?

Oph. O, my lord, my lord, I have been so affrighted !

Pol. With what, i' the name of God ?

Oph. My lord, as I was sewing in my closet,
        Lord Hamlet, with his doublet all unbrac'd,
        No hat upon his head, his stockings foul'd,
        Ungarter'd and down-gyved to his ancle,
        Pale as his shirt, his knees knocking each other,   80
        And with a look so piteous in purport
        As if he had been loosed out of hell
        To speak of horrors, he comes before me.

Pol. Mad for thy love ?

Oph.   My lord, I do not know,
        But truly I do fear it.

Pol.   What said he ?

Oph. He took me by the wrist and held me hard ;
        Then goes he to the length of all his arm,
        And with his other hand thus o'er his brow,
        He falls to such perusal of my face
        As 'a would draw it.   Long stay'd he so ;   90
        At last, a little shaking of mine arm,

And thrice his head thus waving up and down,
He rais'd a sigh so piteous and profound
As it did seem to shatter all his bulk,
And end his being : that done, he lets me go,
And with his head over his shoulder turn'd,
He seem'd to find his way without his eyes,
For out o' doors he went without their helps,
And to the last bended their light on me.

Pol. Come, go with me ; I will go seek the king.   100
This is the very ecstasy of love,
Whose violent property fordoes itself
And leads the will to desperate undertakings
As oft as any passion under heaven
That does afflict our natures.   I am sorry.
What, have you given him any hard words of late ?

Oph. No, my good lord, but, as you did command,
I did repel his letters, and denied
His access to me.

Pol.   That hath made him mad.
I am sorry that with better heed and judgement   110
I had not coted him : I fear'd he did but trifle
And meant to wreck thee ; but beshrew my jealousy !
By heaven, it is as proper to our age
To cast beyond ourselves in our opinions
As it is common for the younger sort

To lack discretion.   Come, go we to the king:
This must be known, which, being kept close, might
    move
More grief to hide than hate to utter love.
Come.   *Exeunt*

SCENE II

A room in the castle

*Flourish.   Enter King, Queen, Rosencrantz, Guildenstern,
and Attendants*

Ki. Welcome, dear Rosencrantz and Guildenstern!
Moreover that we much did long to see you,
The need we have to use you did provoke
Our hasty sending.   Something have you heard
Of Hamlet's transformation; so call it,
Sith nor the exterior nor the inward man
Resembles that it was.   What it should be,
More than his father's death, that thus hath put him
So much from the understanding of himself,
I cannot dream of: I entreat you both,
That, being of so young days brought up with him
And sith so neighbour'd to his youth and haviour,
That you vouchsafe your rest here in our court

Some little time, so by your companies
To draw him on to pleasures, and to gather
So much as from occasion you may glean,
Whether aught to us unknown afflicts him thus,
That open'd lies within our remedy.

u. Good gentlemen, he hath much talk'd of you,
And sure I am two men there is not living   20
To whom he more adheres.   If it will please you
To show us so much gentry and good will
As to expend your time with us a while,
For the supply and profit of our hope,
Your visitation shall receive such thanks
As fits a king's remembrance.

os.   Both your majesties
Might, by the sovereign power you have of us,
Put your dread pleasures more into command
Than to entreaty.

ui.   But we both obey,
And here give up ourselves, in the full bent,   30
To lay our service freely at your feet
To be commanded.

. Thanks, Rosencrantz and gentle Guildenstern.

. Thanks, Guildenstern and gentle Rosencrantz :
And I beseech you instantly to visit
My too much changed son.   Go, some of you,

And bring these gentlemen where Hamlet is.

Gui. Heavens make our presence and our practices
 Pleasant and helpful to him !

Qu.   Ay, amen !

  Exeunt Rosencrantz, Guildenstern, and some Attendants
       Enter Polonius

Pol. The ambassadors from Norway, my good lord,
 Are joyfully return'd.   I do think

Ki. Thou still hast been the father of good news.

Pol. Have I, my lord ? Assure you, my good liege,
 I hold my duty as I hold my soul,
 Both to my God, and to my gracious king :
 And I do think, or else this brain of mine
 Hunts not the trail of policy so sure
 As it hath us'd to do, that I have found
 The very cause of Hamlet's lunacy.

Ki. O, speak of that ; that do I long to hear.

Pol. Give first admittance to the ambassadors ;
 My news shall be the fruit to that great feast.

Ki. Thyself do grace to them, and bring them in.

          Exit Polonius

He tells me, my dear Gertrude, he hath found
The head and source of all your son's distemper.

Qu. I doubt it is no other but the main,
 His father's death, and our o'erhasty marriage.

i. Well, we shall sift him.

  Re-enter Polonius, with Voltimand and Cornelius

              Welcome, my good friends !
  Say, Voltimand, what from our brother Norway ?

ol. Most fair return of greetings and desires.   60
  Upon our first, he sent out to suppress
  His nephew's levies, which to him appear'd
  To be a preparation 'gainst the Polack,
  But better look'd into, he truly found
  It was against your highness ; whereat griev'd
  That so his sickness, age, and impotence
  Was falsely borne in hand, sends out arrests
  On Fortinbras, which he in brief obeys,
  Receives rebuke from Norway, and in fine
  Makes vow before his uncle never more   70
  To give the assay of arms against your majesty.
  Whereon old Norway, overcome with joy,
  Gives him threescore thousand crowns in annual fee
  And his commission to employ those soldiers,
  So levied as before, against the Polack,
  With an entreaty, herein further shown,

                     Giving a paper

  That it might please you to give quiet pass
  Through your dominions for this enterprise,
  On such regards of safety and allowance

As therein are set down.

Ki.   It likes us well,
And at our more consider'd time we'll read,
Answer, and think upon this business.
Meantime, we thank you for your well-took labour:
Go to your rest; at night we'll feast together:
Most welcome home!

> *Exeunt Voltimand and Cornelius*

Pol.   This business is well ended.
My liege, and madam, to expostulate
What majesty should be, what duty is,
Why day is day, night night, and time is time,
Were nothing but to waste night, day, and time.
Therefore, for brevity is the soul of wit
And tediousness the limbs and outward flourishes,
I will be brief; your noble son is mad:
Mad call I it, for, to define true madness,
What is't but to be nothing else but mad?
But let that go.

Qu.   More matter, with less art.

Pol. Madam, I swear I use no art at all.
That he is mad, 'tis true: 'tis true 'tis pity,
And pity 'tis 'tis true: a foolish figure;
But farewell it, for I will use no art.
Mad let us grant him then, and now remains

That we find out the cause of this effect,
Or rather say, the cause of this defect,
For this effect defective comes by cause :
Thus it remains, and the remainder thus.
Perpend ;
I have a daughter,—have while she is mine,—
Who in her duty and obedience, mark,
Hath given me this : now gather and surmise.

Reads

' To the celestial and my soul's idol, the most
beautified Ophelia,'—   110
That 's an ill phrase, a vile phrase ; ' beautified ' is a
vile phrase ; but you shall hear.   *Reads*
Thus—'in her excellent white bosom, these,' &c.

Qu. Came this from Hamlet to her?

Pol. Good madam, stay awhile, I will be faithful.

Reads

> ' Doubt thou the stars are fire,
>   Doubt that the sun doth move,
>   Doubt truth to be a liar,
>   But never doubt I love.

' O dear Ophelia, I am ill at these numbers, I have not 120
art to reckon my groans, but that I love thee best, O
most best believe it ; Adieu.

51

'Thine evermore, most dear lady, whilst this
machine is to him,   HAMLET.'

This in obedience hath my daughter shown me,
And, more above, hath his solicitings,
As they fell out by time, by means, and place,
All given to mine ear.

Ki.   But how hath she
Receiv'd his love ?

Pol.   What do you think of me ?

Ki. As of a man faithful and honourable.   13

Pol. I would fain prove so, but what might you think,
When I had seen this hot love on the wing,
As I perceiv'd it (I must tell you that)
Before my daughter told me, what might you,
Or my dear majesty your queen here, think,
If I had play'd the desk, or table-book,
Or given my heart a winking, mute and dumb,
Or look'd upon this love with idle sight,
What might you think ? No, I went round to
work,
And my young mistress thus I did bespeak :   14
'Lord Hamlet is a prince out of thy star ;
This must not be :' and then I prescripts gave her,
That she should lock herself from his resort,
Admit no messengers, receive no tokens ;

Which done, she took the fruits of my advice;
And he repelled, a short tale to make,
Fell into a sadness, then into a fast,
Thence to a watch, thence into a weakness,
Thence to a lightness, and by this declension
Into the madness wherein now he raves   150
And all we mourn for.

Ki. Do you think this?

Qu.   It may be, very like.

Pol. Hath there been such a time, I 'ld fain know that,
That I have positively said ''tis so,'
When it prov'd otherwise?

Ki.   Not that I know.

Pol. (*pointing to his head and shoulder*) Take this from this,
      if this be otherwise:
If circumstances lead me, I will find
Where truth is hid, though it were hid indeed
Within the centre.

Ki.   How may we try it further?

Pol. You know, sometimes he walks four hours together 160
Here in the lobby.

Qu.   So he does, indeed.

Pol. At such a time I 'll loose my daughter to him:
Be you and I behind an arras then;
Mark the encounter: if he love her not,

F   53

And be not from his reason fall'n thereon,
Let me be no assistant for a state,
But keep a farm and carters.

Ki.   We will try it.

Qu. But look where sadly the poor wretch comes reading.

Pol. Away, I do beseech you, both away: ~~stand back~~
I 'll board him presently; O, give me leave.   170

> *Exeunt King, Queen, and Attendants*
> *Enter Hamlet, reading*

How does my good Lord Hamlet?

Ham. Well, God-a-mercy.

Pol. Do you know me, my lord?

Ham. Excellent {excellent} well, you are a fishmonger.

Pol. Not I, my lord.

Ham. Then I would you were so honest a man.

Pol. Honest, my lord?

Ham. Ay, sir; to be honest, as this world goes, is to be one man pick'd out of ten thousand.

Pol. That 's very true, my lord.   180

Ham. For if the sun breed maggots in a dead dog, being a good kissing carrion—Have you a daughter?   †

Pol. I have, my lord.

Ham. Let her not walk i' the sun: conception is a blessing; but as your daughter may conceive,—friend, look to 't.

Pol. (*aside*) How say you by that? Still harping on my
    daughter: yet he knew me not at first, 'a said I was
    a fishmonger: 'a is far gone {, far gone}: and truly
    in my youth I suffer'd much extremity for love; 190
    very near this. I 'll speak to him again. What do
    you read, my lord?

Ham. Words, words, words.

Pol. What is the matter, my lord?

Ham. Between who?

Pol. I mean, the matter that you read, my lord.

Ham. Slanders, sir: for the satirical rogue says here that
    old men have grey beards, that their faces are wrinkled,
    their eyes purging thick amber and plum-tree gum,
    and that they have a plentiful lack of wit, together 200
    with most weak hams: all which, sir, though I most
    powerfully and potently believe, yet I hold it not
    honesty to have it thus set down; for yourself, sir,
    shall grow old as I am, if like a crab you could go
    backward.

Pol. (*aside*) Though this be madness, yet there is method
    in 't.—Will you walk out of the air, my lord?

Ham. Into my grave.

Pol. Indeed, that 's out of the air. (*aside*) How pregnant
    sometimes his replies are! a happiness that often 210
    madness hits on, which reason and sanity could

not so prosperously be deliver'd of. I will leave
him, {and suddenly contrive the means of meeting
between him} and my daughter.—My lord, I will
take my leave of you.

Ham. You cannot take from me any thing that I will not
more willingly part withal : except my life, [except
my life, except] my life.

Pol. Fare you well, my lord.

Ham. These tedious old fools !   220

Re-enter Rosencrantz and Guildenstern

Pol. You go to seek the Lord Hamlet ; there he is.

Ros. (*to Polonius*) God save you, sir !   *Exit Polonius*

Gui. My honour'd lord !

Ros. My most dear lord !

Ham. My excellent good friends ! How dost thou,
Guildenstern ? Ah, Rosencrantz ! Good lads, how
do you both ?

Ros. As the indifferent children of the earth.

Gui. Happy, in that we are not over-happy ;
On Fortune's cap we are not the very button.   230

Ham. Nor the soles of her shoe ?

Ros. Neither, my lord.

Ham. Then you live about her waist, or in the middle of
her favours.

Gui. Faith, her privates we.

Ham. In the secret parts of Fortune ?   O, most true ; she
    is a strumpet.   What news ?

Ros. None, my lord, but the world's grown honest.

Ham. Then is doomsday near : but your news is not true.
    {Let me question more in particular : what have 240
    you, my good friends, deserv'd at the hands of
    Fortune, that she sends you to prison hither ?

Gui. Prison, my lord ?

Ham. Denmark 's a prison.

Ros. Then is the world one.

Ham. A goodly one ; in which there are many confines,
    wards and dungeons ; Denmark being one o' the
    worst.

Ros. We think not so, my lord.

Ham. Why, then 'tis none to you ; for there is nothing 250
    either good or bad, but thinking makes it so : to
    me it is a prison.

Ros. Why then your ambition makes it one ; 'tis too
    narrow for your mind.

Ham. O God, I could be bounded in a nut-shell, and
    count myself a king of infinite space, were it not that
    I have bad dreams.

Gui. Which dreams indeed are ambition ; for the very
    substance of the ambitious is merely the shadow
    of a dream.   260

Ham. A dream itself is but a shadow.

Ros. Truly, and I hold ambition of so airy and light a
quality that it is but a shadow's shadow.

Ham. Then are our beggars bodies, and our monarchs
and outstretch'd heroes the beggars' shadows. Shall
we to the court ? for, by my fay, I cannot reason.

Ros.
Gui. } We 'll wait upon you.

Ham. No such matter : I will not sort you with the rest of
my servants ; for, to speak to you like an honest man,
I am most dreadfully attended.} But, in the beaten 270
way of friendship, what make you at Elsinore ?

Ros. To visit you, my lord, no other occasion.

Ham. Beggar that I am, I am even poor in thanks ; but
I thank you : and sure, dear friends, my thanks are
too dear a halfpenny. Were you not sent for ? is it
your own inclining ? is it a free visitation ? Come,
come, deal justly with me : come, come ; nay, speak.

Gui. What should we say, my lord ?

Ham. Any thing but to the purpose. You were sent
for, and there is a kind of confession in your looks, 280
which your modesties have not craft enough to
colour : I know the good king and queen have sent
for you.

Ros. To what end, my lord ?

Ham. That you must teach me.   But let me conjure you,
by the rights of our fellowship, by the consonancy
of our youth, by the obligation of our ever-preserv'd
love, and by what more dear a better proposer can
charge you withal, be even and direct with me,
whether you were sent for, or no.   290

Ros. (*aside to Guil.*) What say you ?

Ham. (*aside*) Nay then, I have an eye of you.—If you
love me, hold not off.

Gui. My lord, we were sent for.

Ham. I will tell you why ; so shall my anticipation prevent your discovery, and your secrecy to the king
and queen moult no feather.   I have of late—but
wherefore I know not—lost all my mirth, forgone
all custom of exercises ; and indeed it goes so heavily
with my disposition that this goodly frame, the   300
earth, seems to me a sterile promontory, this most
excellent canopy, the air, look you, this brave o'er-
hanging [firmament], this majestical roof fretted with
golden fire, why, it appeareth nothing to me but a
foul and pestilent congregation of vapours.   What
piece of work is a man, how noble in reason, how
infinite in faculties, in form and moving how express and admirable, in action how like an angel, in
apprehension how like a god ; the beauty of the

world; the paragon of animals; and yet, to me, 310
what is this quintessence of dust? man delights not
me, nor women neither, though by your smiling you
seem to say so.

Ros. My lord, there was no such stuff in my thoughts.

Ham. Why did ye laugh then, when I said ' man delights
not me ' ?

Ros. To think, my lord, if you delight not in man, what
lenten entertainment the players shall receive from
you : we coted them on the way ; and hither are they
coming, to offer you service. 320

Ham. He that plays the king shall be welcome; his majesty
shall have tribute of me; the adventurous knight
shall use his foil and target ; the lover shall not sigh
gratis ; the humorous man shall end his part in peace ;
{the clown shall make those laugh whose lungs are
tickle o' the sere,} and the lady shall say her mind
freely, or the blank verse shall halt for 't. What
players are they ?

Ros. Even those you were wont to take such delight in,
the tragedians of the city. 330

Ham. How chances it they travel ? their residence, both
in reputation and profit, was better both ways.

Ros. I think their inhibition comes by the means of the late †
innovation.

Ham. Do they hold the same estimation they did when I
was in the city? are they so follow'd?

Ros. No, indeed, are they not.

{*Ham.* How comes it? do they grow rusty?

Ros. Nay, their endeavour keeps in the wonted pace: but
there is, sir, an eyrie of children, little eyases, that cry   340
out on the top of question and are most tyrannically
clapped for 't: these are now the fashion, and so
berattle the common stages—so they call them—that
many wearing rapiers are afraid of goose-quills, and
dare scarce come thither.

Ham. What, are they children? who maintains 'em? how
are they escoted?   Will they pursue the quality no
longer than they can sing? will they not say after-
wards, if they should grow themselves to common
players,—as it is most like, if their means are no   350
better,—their writers do them wrong, to make them
exclaim against their own succession?

Ros. Faith, there has been much to do on both sides, and
the nation holds it no sin to tarre them to con-
troversy: there was for a while no money bid for
argument unless the poet and the player went to
cuffs in the question.

Ham. Is 't possible?

Gui. O, there has been much throwing about of brains.

Ham. Do the boys carry it away?

Ros. Ay, that they do, my lord; Hercules and his load too.}

Ham. It is not very strange, for my uncle is king of
Denmark, and those that would make mouths at him
while my father lived, give twenty, forty, fifty, a
hundred ducats a-piece, for his picture in little.
'Sblood, there is something in this more than natural,
if philosophy could find it out.

Flourish of trumpets within

Gui. There are the players.

Ham. Gentlemen, you are welcome to Elsinore. Your
hands, come then: the appurtenance of welcome is 370
fashion and ceremony: let me comply with you in
this garb, lest my extent to the players, which, I tell
you, must show fairly outwards, should more appear
like entertainment than yours. You are welcome:
but my uncle-father and aunt-mother are deceived.

Gui. In what, my dear lord?

Ham. I am but mad north-north-west: when the wind
is southerly I know a hawk from a handsaw.   †

Re-enter Polonius

Pol. Well be with you, gentlemen!

Ham. Hark you, Guildenstern, and you too, at each 38
ear a hearer; that great baby you see there is not yet
out of his swaddling clouts.

62

Ros. Haply he is the second time come to them, for they
say an old man is twice a child.

Ham. I will prophesy ; he comes to tell me of the players ;
mark it.   You say right, sir : o' Monday morning ;
'twas then indeed.

Pol. My lord, I have news to tell you.

Ham. My lord, I have news to tell you.   When Roscius
was an actor in Rome,—   390

Pol. The actors are come hither, my lord.

Ham. Buz, buz !

Pol. Upon my honour,—

Ham. Then came each actor on his ass,—

Pol. The best actors in the world, either for tragedy,
comedy, history, pastoral, pastoral-comical, historical-pastoral, {tragical-historical, tragical-comical-
historical-pastoral,} scene individible, or poem un-
limited : Seneca cannot be too heavy, nor Plautus
too light for the law of writ, and the liberty : these 400
are the only men.

Ham. O Jephthah, judge of Israel, what a treasure hadst
thou !

Pol. What a treasure had he, my lord ?

Ham. Why,

> ' One fair daughter, and no more,
>   The which he loved passing well.'

Pol. (*aside*) Still on my daughter.

Ham. Am I not i' the right, old Jephthah?

Pol. If you call me Jephthah, my lord, I have a daughter 41(
that I love passing well.

Ham. Nay, that follows not.

Pol. What follows then, my lord?

Ham. Why,

'As by lot, God wot,'

and then you know,

'It came to pass, as most like it was,'—
the first row of the pious chanson will show you
more; for look where my abridgement comes.

Enter the Players

You are welcome, masters, welcome all. I am glad 42
to see thee well. Welcome, good friends. O, old
friend! Why, thy face is valanc'd since I saw thee
last; com'st thou to beard me in Denmark? What,
my young lady and mistress! By'r lady, your lady-
ship is nearer to heaven than when I saw you last by
the altitude of a chopine. Pray God your voice,
like a piece of uncurrent gold, be not crack'd within
the ring. Masters, you are all welcome. We'll
e'en to't like French falconers, fly at any thing we
see: we'll have a speech straight: come, give us a 4:
taste of your quality. come, a passionate speech.

First Pla. What speech, my good lord?

Ham. I heard thee speak me a speech once, but it was
never acted, or, if it was, not above once; for the
play, I remember, pleas'd not the million; 'twas
caviare to the general: but it was—as I received it,
and others, whose judgements in such matters cried
in the top of mine—an excellent play, well digested
in the scenes, set down with as much modesty as
cunning. I remember, one said there were no sallets 440
in the lines, to make the matter savoury, nor no matter
in the phrase that might indict the author of affection;
but call'd it an honest method, [as wholesome as
sweet, and by very much more handsome than
fine.] One speech in't I chiefly lov'd: 'twas
Æneas' talk to Dido, and thereabout of it especially,
when he speaks of Priam's slaughter: if it live
in your memory, begin at this line; let me see, let
me see;

' The rugged Pyrrhus, like th' Hyrcanian beast,'— 450
'Tis not so: it begins with ' Pyrrhus.'

' The rugged Pyrrhus, he whose sable arms,
Black as his purpose, did the night resemble,
When he lay couched in the ominous horse,
Hath now this dread and black complexion smear'd,
With heraldry more dismal head to foot;

65

Now is he total gules, horridly trick'd
With blood of fathers, mothers, daughters, sons,
Bak'd and impasted with the parching streets
That lend a tyrannous and a damned light   460
To their lord's murder : roasted in wrath and fire,
And thus o'er-sized with coagulate gore,
With eyes like carbuncles, the hellish Pyrrhus
Old grandsire Priam seeks.'
So, proceed you.

Pol. 'Fore God, my lord, well spoken, with good accent
and good discretion.

First Pla.   ' Anon he finds him
Striking too short at Greeks ; his antique sword,
Rebellious to his arm, lies where it falls,
Repugnant to command : unequal match'd,   470
Pyrrhus at Priam drives, in rage strikes wide,
But with the whiff and wind of his fell sword
The unnerved father falls.   {Then senseless Ilium,}
Seeming to feel this blow, with flaming top
Stoops to his base ; and with a hideous crash
Takes prisoner Pyrrhus' ear, for, lo ! his sword,
Which was declining on the milky head
Of reverend Priam, seem'd i' the air to stick ;
So, as a painted tyrant, Pyrrhus stood,
And like a neutral to his will and matter,   48

Did nothing.

But as we often see, against some storm,
A silence in the heavens, the rack stand still,
The bold winds speechless, and the orb below
As hush as death, anon the dreadful thunder
Doth rend the region, so after Pyrrhus' pause
A roused vengeance sets him new a-work;
And never did the Cyclops' hammers fall
On Mars's armour, forg'd for proof eterne,
With less remorse than Pyrrhus' bleeding sword   490
Now falls on Priam.

Out, out, thou strumpet, Fortune!   All you gods,
In general synod take away her power,
Break all the spokes and fellies from her wheel,
And bowl the round nave down the hill of heaven
As low as to the fiends!'

Pol. This is too long.

Ham. It shall to the barber's, with your beard.

Prithee, say on: he's for a jig, or a tale of bawdry,
or he sleeps: say on, come to Hecuba.   500

First Pla. 'But who, ah! woe, had seen the mobled
queen—'

Ham. 'The mobled queen?'

Pol. That's good; {'mobled queen' is good.}

First Pla. 'Run barefoot up and down, threatening the flames

With bisson rheum, a clout upon that head
Where late the diadem stood, and for a robe,
About her lank and all o'er-teemed loins,
A blanket in the alarm of fear caught up :
Who this had seen, with tongue in venom steep'd   510
'Gainst Fortune's state would treason have pronounc'd ;
But if the gods themselves did see her then,
When she saw Pyrrhus make malicious sport
In mincing with his sword her husband's limbs,
The instant burst of clamour that she made,
Unless things mortal move them not at all,
Would have made milch the burning eyes of heaven
And passion in the gods.'

Pol. Look, whether he has not turn'd his colour, and has
tears in 's eyes.   Prithee, no more.   520

Ham. 'Tis well ; I 'll have thee speak out the rest of this
soon.   Good my lord, will you see the players well
bestow'd ?   Do you hear, let them be well us'd, for
they are the abstract and brief chronicles of the time :
after your death you were better have a bad epitaph
than their ill report while you live.

Pol. My lord, I will use them according to their desert.

Ham. God's bodkin, man, much better : use every man
after his desert, and who shall 'scape whipping ?
Use them after your own honour and dignity ; the   530

68

less they deserve, the more merit is in your bounty.
Take them in.

Pol. Come, sirs.

Ham. Follow him, friends : we 'll hear a play to-morrow.
(*exit Polonius with all the Players but the First.*) Dost
thou hear me, old friend ; can you play the Murder
of Gonzago ?

First Pla. Ay, my lord.

Ham. We 'll ha 't to-morrow night. You could, for
need, study a speech of some dozen lines or sixteen 540
lines, which I would set down and insert in 't, could
you not ?

First Pla. Ay, my lord.

Ham. Very well. Follow that lord, and look you mock
him not. [*exit First Player.*] My good friends, I 'll
leave you till night : you are welcome to Elsinore.

Ros. Good my lord !

Ham. Ay, so, good bye to you !   [*exeunt Rosencrantz and
Guildenstern.*] Now I am alone.

O, what a rogue and peasant slave am I !
Is it not monstrous that this player here,   550
But in a fiction, in a dream of passion,
Could force his soul so to his own conceit
That from her working all the visage wann'd,
Tears in his eyes, distraction in 's aspect,

G   69

A broken voice, and his whole function suiting
With forms to his conceit ? and all for nothing,
For Hecuba !
What 's Hecuba to him, or he to her,   †
That he should weep for her ?   What would he do,
Had he the motive and the cue for passion   560
That I have ?   He would drown the stage with tears
And cleave the general ear with horrid speech,
Make mad the guilty, and appal the free,
Confound the ignorant, and amaze indeed
The very faculties of eyes and ears.
Yet I,
A dull and muddy-mettled rascal, peak,
Like John-a-dreams, unpregnant of my cause,
And can say nothing : no, not for a king,
Upon whose property and most dear life   570
A damn'd defeat was made.   Am I a coward,
Who calls me villain, breaks my pate across,
Plucks off my beard, and blows it in my face,
Tweaks me by the nose, gives me the lie i' the throat,
As deep as to the lungs ? who does me this ?
Ha !
'Swounds, I should take it : for it cannot be
But I am pigeon-liver'd, and lack gall
To make oppression bitter, or ere this

I should ha' fatted all the region kites   580
With this slave's offal: bloody, bawdy villain,
Remorseless, treacherous, lecherous, kindless villain!
{O, vengeance!}
Why, what an ass am I! This is most brave,
That I, the son of a dear father murder'd,
Prompted to my revenge by heaven and hell,
Must like a whore unpack my heart with words,
And fall a-cursing like a very drab,
A stallion!
Fie upon 't! foh! About, my brains! [Hum,] I
        have heard   590
That guilty creatures, sitting at a play,
Have by the very cunning of the scene
Been struck so to the soul, that presently
They have proclaim'd their malefactions;
For murder, though it have no tongue, will speak
With most miraculous organ. I 'll have these players
Play something like the murder of my father
Before mine uncle, I 'll observe his looks,
I 'll tent him to the quick; if 'a do blench,
I know my course. The spirit that I have seen   600
May be a devil, and the devil hath power
To assume a pleasing shape; yea, and perhaps
Out of my weakness, and my melancholy,

71

As he is very potent with such spirits,
Abuses me to damn me ; I 'll have grounds
More relative than this ; the play 's the thing
Wherein I 'll catch the conscience of the king.

Exit

Act Third

SCENE I

The next day

A room in the castle

*Enter King, Queen, Polonius, Ophelia, Rosencrantz,
and Guildenstern*

Ki. And can you, by no drift of conference,
Get from him why he puts on this confusion,
Grating so harshly all his days of quiet
With turbulent and dangerous lunacy ?

Ros. He does confess he feels himself distracted,
But from what cause 'a will by no means speak.

Gui. Nor do we find him forward to be sounded,
But, with a crafty madness, keeps aloof,
When we would bring him on to some confession
Of his true state.

Qu.   Did he receive you well ?   10

Ros. Most like a gentleman.

Gui. But with much forcing of his disposition.

Ros. Niggard of question, but of our demands   †
      Most free in his reply.

Qu.   Did you assay him
      To any pastime ?

Ros. Madam, it so fell out that certain players
      We o'er-raught on the way ; of these we told him,
      And there did seem in him a kind of joy
      To hear of it : they are here about the court,
      And, as I think, they have already order   20
      This night to play before him.

Pol.   'Tis most true,
      And he beseech'd me to entreat your majesties
      To hear and see the matter.

Ki. With all my heart ; and it doth much content me
      To hear him so inclin'd.
      Good gentlemen, give him a further edge,
      And drive his purpose into these delights.

Ros. We shall, my lord.

            Exeunt Rosencrantz and Guildenstern

Ki.   Sweet Gertrude, leave us two,
      For we have closely sent for Hamlet hither,
      That he, as 'twere by accident, may here   30

Affront Ophelia : her father and myself,
{Lawful espials,}
We'll so bestow ourselves that, seeing unseen,
We may of their encounter frankly judge,
And gather by him, as he is behav'd,
If 't be the affliction of his love or no
That thus he suffers for.

Qu.   I shall obey you.
And for your part, Ophelia, I do wish
That your good beauties be the happy cause
Of Hamlet's wildness ; so shall I hope your virtues   40
Will bring him to his wonted way again,
To both your honours.

Oph. *down stage* Madam, I wish it may. *Exit Queen*
Pol. Ophelia, walk you here. Gracious, so please you, *to R*
We will bestow ourselves. (*to Ophelia*) Read on this
          book,
That show of such an exercise may colour
Your loneliness. We are oft to blame in this,—
'Tis too much prov'd—that with devotion's visage
And pious action we do sugar o'er
The devil himself.

Ki.   (*aside*) O, 'tis too true !
How smart a lash that speech doth give my conscience !
The harlot's cheek, beautied with plastering art,   51

74

Is not more ugly to the thing that helps it
Than is my deed to my most painted word:
O heavy burthen!

Pol. I hear him coming: let's withdraw, my lord.

Exeunt King and Polonius

Enter Hamlet

Ham. To be, or not to be, that is the question;
Whether 'tis nobler in the mind to suffer
The slings and arrows of outrageous fortune,
Or to take arms against a sea of troubles,
And by opposing, end them.   To die; to sleep,   60
No more, and by a sleep to say we end
The heart-ache, and the thousand natural shocks
That flesh is heir to; 'tis a consummation
Devoutly to be wish'd, to die, to sleep;
To sleep; perchance to dream; ay, there's the rub;
For in that sleep of death what dreams may come,
When we have shuffled off this mortal coil,
Must give us pause; there's the respect
That makes calamity of so long life:
For who would bear the whips and scorns of time,   70
The oppressor's wrong, the proud man's contumely,
The pangs of despis'd love, the law's delay,
The insolence of office, and the spurns
That patient merit of the unworthy takes,

When he himself might his quietus make
With a bare bodkin? who would fardels bear,
To grunt and sweat under a weary life,
But that the dread of something after death,
The undiscover'd country, from whose bourn
No traveller returns, puzzles the will,   80
And makes us rather bear those ills we have
Than fly to others that we know not of?
Thus conscience does make cowards {of us all,}
And thus the native hue of resolution
Is sicklied o'er with the pale cast of thought,
And enterprises of great pitch and moment
With this regard their currents turn awry
And lose the name of action.   Soft you now,
The fair Ophelia!   Nymph, in thy orisons
Be all my sins remember'd.

Oph.   Good my lord,   90
How does your honour for this many a day?

Ham. I humbly thank you, well, {well, well.}

Oph. My lord, I have remembrances of yours,
That I have longed long to re-deliver;
I pray you now receive them.

Ham.   No, not I;
I never gave you aught.

Oph. My honour'd lord, you know right well you did,

And with them words of so sweet breath compos'd
As made these things more rich : their perfume lost,
Take these again ; for to the noble mind   100
Rich gifts wax poor when givers prove unkind.
There, my lord.

Ham. Ha, ha ! are you honest ?

Oph. My lord ?

Ham. Are you fair ?

Oph. What means your lordship ?

Ham. That if you be honest and fair, your honesty should
admit no discourse to your beauty.

Oph. Could beauty, my lord, have better converse than   †
with honesty ?   110

Ham. Ay, truly ; for the power of beauty will sooner
transform honesty from what it is to a bawd than the
force of honesty can translate beauty into his likeness :
this was sometime a paradox, but now the time gives
it proof.   I did love you once.

Oph. Indeed, my lord, you made me believe so.

Ham. You should not have believ'd me, for virtue cannot
so inoculate our old stock but we shall relish of it :
I lov'd you not.

Oph. I was the more deceiv'd.   120

Ham. Get thee to a nunnery ; why wouldst thou be a
breeder of sinners ?   I am myself indifferent honest,

but yet I could accuse me of such things that it were
better my mother had not borne me: I am very
proud, revengeful, ambitious, with more offences
at my beck than I have thoughts to put them in,
imagination to give them shape, or time to act
them in.   What should such fellows as I do crawling
between earth and heaven?   We are arrant knaves,
believe none of us, go thy ways to a nunnery. 130
Where's your father?

Oph. At home, my lord.

Ham. Let the doors be shut upon him, that he may play
the fool no where but in's own house.   Farewell.

Oph. O, help him, you sweet heavens!

Ham. If thou dost marry, I'll give thee this plague for
thy dowry: be thou as chaste as ice, as pure as
snow, thou shalt not escape calumny.   Get thee to
a nunnery, farewell.   Or, if thou wilt needs marry,
marry a fool, for wise men know well enough what 140
monsters you make of them.   To a nunnery, go,
and quickly too, farewell.

Oph. Heavenly powers restore him!

Ham. I have heard of your paintings well enough; God
hath given you one face, and you make yourselves
another: you jig and amble; an you list you nick-
name God's creatures, and make your wantonness

ignorance.   Go to, I'll no more on't, it hath made
me mad.   I say we will have no more marriage;
those that are married already, all but one shall live,   150
the rest shall keep as they are.   To a nunnery, go.

Exit

Oph. O, what a noble mind is here o'erthrown!
   The courtier's, soldier's, scholar's, eye, tongue,
      sword,
   The expectancy and rose of the fair state,
   The glass of fashion, and the mould of form,
   The observ'd of all observers, quite, quite down,
   And I of ladies most deject and wretched,
   That suck'd the honey of his music'd vows;
   Now see that noble and most sovereign reason,
   Like sweet bells jangled out of time, and harsh,   †
   That unmatch'd form, and stature of blown youth,   161
   Blasted with ecstasy: O, woe is me,
   To have seen what I have seen, see what I see!

   Re-enter King and Polonius   out

Ki. Love! his affections do not that way tend,
   Nor what he spake, though it lack'd form a little,
   Was not like madness.   There's something in his soul
   O'er which his melancholy sits on brood,
   And I do doubt the hatch and the disclose
   Will be some danger: which [for] to prevent,

I have in quick determination 170
Thus set it down :—he shall with speed to England,
For the demand of our neglected tribute :
Haply the seas, and countries different,
With variable objects, shall expel
This something-settled matter in his heart,
Whereon his brains still beating puts him thus
From fashion of himself.   What think you on 't ?

Pol. It shall do well : but yet do I believe
The origin and commencement of his grief *to her*
Sprung from neglected love.   How now, Ophelia ? 180
You need not tell us what Lord Hamlet said,
We heard it all.   My lord, do as you please ; *to steps*
But if you hold it fit, after the play,
Let his queen mother all alone entreat him
To show his grief ; let her be round with him ;
And I 'll be plac'd, so please you, in the ear
Of all their conference.   If she find him not,
To England send him ; or confine him where
Your wisdom best shall think.

Ki.   It shall be so :
Madness in great ones must not unwatch'd go. 19

Exeunt

SCENE II

A hall in the castle

Enter Hamlet and three of the Players

Ham. Speak the speech, I pray you, as I pronounc'd it
to you, trippingly on the tongue; but if you mouth
it as many of our players do, I had as lief the town-
crier spoke my lines; nor do not saw the air too
much with your hand thus, but use all gently, for in
the very torrent, tempest, and, as I may say, whirl-
wind of your passion, you must acquire and beget
a temperance, that may give it smoothness. O, it
offends me to the soul to hear a robustious periwig-
pated fellow tear a passion to tatters, to very rags,   10
to split the ears of the groundlings, who for the most
part are capable of nothing but inexplicable dumb-
shows, and noise: I would have such a fellow
whipp'd for o'erdoing Termagant; it out-herods
Herod: pray you, avoid it.

First Pla. I warrant your honour.

Ham. Be not too tame neither, but let your own discretion be your tutor, suit the action to the word, the
word to the action, with this special observance,
that you o'erstep not the modesty of nature: for   20

anything so o'erdone is from the purpose of playing, whose end, both at the first, and now, was and is, to hold as 'twere the mirror up to nature, to show virtue her {own} feature, scorn her own image, and the very age and body of the time his form and pressure. Now this overdone, or come tardy off, though it makes the unskilful laugh, cannot but make the judicious grieve, the censure of which one must in your allowance o'erweigh a whole theatre of others. O, there be players that I have seen play, 30 and heard others praise, and that highly, not to speak it profanely, that neither having the accent of Christians, nor the gait of Christian, pagan, nor man, have so strutted and bellow'd, that I have thought some of nature's journeymen had made men, and not made them well, they imitated humanity so abhominably.

First Pla. I hope we have reform'd that indifferently with us.

Ham. O, reform it altogether; and let those that play 40 your clowns speak no more than is set down for them: for there be of them that will themselves laugh, to set on some quantity of barren spectators to laugh too, though in the mean time some necessary question of the play be then to be consider'd: that's

villainous, and shows a most pitiful ambition in the
fool that uses it.   Go, make you ready.

Exeunt Players

Enter Polonius, Rosencrantz, and Guildenstern

How now, my lord ? will the king hear this piece of
work ?

Pol. And the queen too, and that presently.   50

Ham. Bid the players make haste.   *Exit Polonius*
Will you two help to hasten them ?

Ros.
Gui. } Ay, my lord.

Exeunt Rosencrantz and Guildenstern

Ham. What ho ! Horatio !

Enter Horatio

Hor. Here, sweet lord, at your service.

Ham. Horatio, thou art e'en as just a man
As e'er my conversation cop'd withal.

Hor. O, my dear lord,—

Ham.   Nay, do not think I flatter,
For what advancement may I hope from thee,
That no revenue hast but thy good spirits,   60
To feed and clothe thee ?   Why should the poor be
flatter'd ?
No, let the candied tongue lick absurd pomp,
And crook the pregnant hinges of the knee

Where thrift may follow fawning.   Dost thou hear?
Since my dear soul was mistress of her choice,
And could of men distinguish her election,
S'hath seal'd thee for herself, for thou hast been
As one, in suffering all, that suffers nothing,
A man that fortune's buffets and rewards
Hast ta'en with equal thanks : and blest are those   7⁰
Whose blood and judgement are so well commedled †
That they are not a pipe for fortune's finger
To sound what stop she please.   Give me that man
That is not passion's slave, and I will wear him
In my heart's core, ay, in my heart of heart,
As I do thee.   Something too much of this.
There is a play to-night before the king ;
One scene of it comes near the circumstance
Which I have told thee of my father's death :
I prithee, when thou seest that act a-foot,   8⁰
Even with the very comment of thy soul
Observe my uncle ; if his occulted guilt
Do not itself unkennel in one speech,
It is a damned ghost that we have seen,
And my imaginations are as foul
As Vulcan's stithy.   Give him heedful note ;
For I mine eyes will rivet to his face,
And after we will both our judgements join

In censure of his seeming.

Hor.   Well, my lord :
If 'a steal aught the whilst this play is playing,   90
And 'scape detecting, I will pay the theft.

Ham. They are coming to the play : I must be idle :
Get you a place.

*Danish march. A flourish. Enter King, Queen, Polonius,
Ophelia, Rosencrantz, Guildenstern, and other Lords
attendant, with the Guard carrying torches*

Ki. How fares our cousin Hamlet ?

Ham. Excellent, i' faith, of the chameleon's dish : I eat
the air, promise-cramm'd : you cannot feed capons
so.

Ki. I have nothing with this answer, Hamlet ; these
words are not mine.

Ham. No, nor mine now. [*to Polonius*] My lord, you   100
play'd once i' the university, you say ?

Pol. That did I, my lord, and was accounted a good
actor.

Ham. What did you enact ?

Pol. I did enact Julius Cæsar, I was killed i' the Capitol,
Brutus kill'd me.

Ham. It was a brute part of him to kill so capital a calf
there.   Be the players ready ?

Ros. Ay, my lord, they stay upon your patience.

Qu. Come hither, my dear Hamlet, sit by me.　　　　110

Ham. No, good mother, here's metal more attractive.

Pol. (*to the King*) O, ho ! do you mark that ?

Ham. Lady, shall I lie in your lap ?

　　　　　　　　　　　　Lying down at Ophelia's feet

Oph. No, my lord.

{*Ham.* I mean, my head upon your lap ?

Oph. Ay, my lord.}

Ham. Do you think I meant country matters ?

Oph. I think nothing, my lord.

Ham. That's a fair thought to lie between maids' legs.

Oph. What is, my lord ?　　　　120

Ham. Nothing.

Oph. You are merry, my lord.

Ham. Who, I ?

Oph. Ay, my lord.

Ham. O God, your only jig-maker. What should a man
　　　do but be merry ? for look you how cheerfully my
　　　mother looks, and my father died within's two hours.

Oph. Nay, 'tis twice two months, my lord.

Ham. So long ? Nay then, let the devil wear black, for
　　　I'll have a suit of sables. O heavens ! die two　130
　　　months ago, and not forgotten yet ? Then there's
　　　hope a great man's memory may outlive his life half
　　　a year : but, by'r lady, 'a must build churches then,

or else shall 'a suffer not thinking on, with the hobby-
horse, whose epitaph is, 'For, O, for, O, the hobby-
horse is forgot.'

The trumpets sound. The dumb-show enters

*Enter a King and a Queen, the Queen embracing him, and he
her. He takes her up, and declines his head upon her
neck: he lies him down upon a bank of flowers: she,
seeing him asleep, leaves him. Anon come in another man,
takes off his crown, kisses it, pours poison in the sleeper's
ears, and leaves him. The Queen returns, finds the King
dead, makes passionate action. The Poisoner with some
three or four come in again, seem to condole with her.
The dead body is carried away. The Poisoner woos the
Queen with gifts: she seems harsh awhile, but in the end
accepts love* Exeunt

Oph. What means this, my lord?

Ham. Marry, this is miching mallecho; it means mischief.

Oph. Belike this show imports the argument of the play.

Enter Prologue

Ham. We shall know by this fellow: the players cannot 140
keep {counsel}; they 'll tell all.

Oph. Will 'a tell us what this show meant?

Ham. Ay, or any show that you will show him: be not
you asham'd to show, he 'll not shame to tell you
what it means.

87

Oph. You are naught, you are naught : I 'll mark the play.

Pro.   For us and for our tragedy,
                 Here stooping to your clemency,
                 We beg your hearing patiently.

Ham. Is this a prologue, or the posy of a ring ?   150

Oph. 'Tis brief, my lord.

Ham. As woman's love.

                 Enter two Players, King and Queen

P.K. Full thirty times hath Phœbus' cart gone round
       Neptune's salt wash and Tellus' orbed ground,
       And thirty dozen moons with borrow'd sheen
       About the world have times twelve thirties been,
       Since love our hearts, and Hymen did our hands,
       Unite commutual in most sacred bands.

P.Q. So many journeys may the sun and moon
       Make us again count o'er ere love be done !   160
       But, woe is me, you are so sick of late,
       So far from cheer and from our former state,
       That I distrust you.   Yet, though I distrust,
       Discomfort you, my lord, it nothing must :
       For [women fear too much, even as they love,   †
       And] women's fear and love hold quantity,
       [Either none,] in neither ought, or in extremity;
       Now, what my love is, proof hath made you know,
       And as my love is siz'd, my fear is so:

[Where love is great, the littlest doubts are fear,   170
Where little fears grow great, great love grows there.]

P.K. Faith, I must leave thee, love, and shortly too ;
My operant powers their functions leave to do :
And thou shalt live in this fair world behind,
Honour'd, belov'd ; and haply one as kind
For husband shalt thou—

P.Q.   O, confound the rest
Such love must needs be treason in my breast :
In second husband let me be accurst,
None wed the second but who kill'd the first.

Ham. (aside) That's wormwood.   180

P.Q. The instances that second marriage move
Are base respects of thrift, but none of love :
A second time I kill my husband dead,
When second husband kisses me in bed.

P.K. I do believe you think what now you speak,
But what we do determine, oft we break.
Purpose is but the slave to memory,
Of violent birth, but poor validity :
Which now, the fruit unripe, sticks on the tree,
But fall unshaken when they mellow be.   190
Most necessary 'tis that we forget
To pay ourselves what to ourselves is debt :
What to ourselves in passion we propose,

The passion ending, doth the purpose lose.
The violence of either, grief or joy,
Their own enactures with themselves destroy:
Where joy most revels, grief doth most lament;
Grief joys, joy grieves, on slender accident.
This world is not for aye, nor 'tis not strange
That even our loves should with our fortunes change:
For 'tis a question left us yet to prove,   201
Whether love lead fortune, or else fortune love.
The great man down, you mark his favourite flies;
The poor advanc'd makes friends of enemies:
And hitherto doth love on fortune tend:
For who not needs shall never lack a friend,
And who in want a hollow friend doth try
Directly seasons him his enemy.
But, orderly to end where I begun,
Our wills and fates do so contrary run,   210
That our devices still are overthrown,
Our thoughts are ours, their ends none of our own:
So think thou wilt no second husband wed,
But die thy thoughts when thy first lord is dead.
P.Q. Nor earth to me give food, nor heaven light!
Sport and repose lock from me day and night!
[To desperation turn my trust and hope,
And anchor's cheer in prison be my scope!]

Each opposite, that blanks the face of joy,
Meet what I would have well and it destroy !   220
Both here and hence pursue me lasting strife,
If, once a widow, ever I be a wife !

Ham. If she should break it now !

P.K. 'Tis deeply sworn.   Sweet, leave me here a while ;
My spirits grow dull, and fain I would beguile
The tedious day with sleep.   *Sleeps*

P.Q.   Sleep rock thy brain,
And never come mischance between us twain !   *Exit*

Ham. Madam, how like you this play ?

Qu. The lady doth protest too much, methinks.

Ham. O, but she 'll keep her word.   230

Ki. Have you heard the argument ?   Is there no offence
in 't ?

Ham. No, no, they do but jest, poison in jest ; no offence
i' the world.

Ki. What do you call the play ?

Ham. The Mouse-trap.   Marry, how ?   Tropically.   This
play is the image of a murder done in Vienna : Gonzago is the duke's name, his wife, Baptista :   you
shall see anon, 'tis a knavish piece of work, but
what of that ?   your majesty, and we that have free   240
souls, it touches us not : let the gall'd jade wince,
our withers are unwrung.

Enter Lucianus

This is one Lucianus, nephew to the king.

Oph. You are as good as a chorus, my lord.

Ham. I could interpret between you and your love, if I could see the puppets dallying.

Oph. You are keen, my lord, you are keen.

Ham. It would cost you a groaning to take off mine edge.

Oph. Still better and worse.

Ham. So you mis-take your husbands.   Begin, murderer, 250 {pox,} leave thy damnable faces, and begin ; come, the croaking raven doth bellow for revenge.

Luc. Thoughts black, hands apt, drugs fit, and time agreeing;

Confederate season, else no creature seeing ;

Thou mixture rank, of midnight weeds collected,

With Hecat's ban thrice blasted, thrice infected,

Thy natural magic, and dire property,

On wholesome life usurps immediately.

Pours the poison into the sleeper's ear

Ham. He poisons him i' the garden for his estate, his name's Gonzago, the story is extant, and written 260 in very choice Italian, you shall see anon how the murderer gets the love of Gonzago's wife.

Oph. The king rises.

{*Ham.* What, frighted with false fire ?}   †

Qu. How fares my lord?

Pol. Give o'er the play.

Ki. Give me some light.   Away!

Pol. Lights, lights, lights.

> *Exeunt all but Hamlet and Horatio*

Ham. Why, let the stricken deer go weep,
>> The hart ungalled play;   270
>>> For some must watch, while some must sleep:
>>>> Thus runs the world away.

Would not this, sir, and a forest of feathers—if the rest of my fortunes turn Turk with me—with Provincial roses on my raz'd shoes, get me a fellowship in a cry of players?

Hor. Half a share.

Ham. A whole one, I.
>> For thou dost know, O Damon dear,
>>> This realm dismantled was   280
>>>> Of Jove himself; and now reigns here
>>>>> A very, very—pacock.   †

Hor. You might have rhym'd.

Ham. O good Horatio, I'll take the ghost's word for a thousand pound.   Didst perceive?

Hor. Very well, my lord.

Ham. Upon the talk of the poisoning?

Hor. I did very well note him.

Ham. Ah, ha! Come, some music! come, the recorders!
　　　For if the king like not the comedy,　　　　　　290
　　　Why then, belike, he likes it not, perdy.
　　Come, some music!

Re-enter Rosencrantz and Guildenstern

Gui. Good my lord, vouchsafe me a word with you.

Ham. Sir, a whole history.

Gui. The king, sir,—

Ham. Ay, sir, what of him?

Gui. Is in his retirement marvellous distemper'd.

Ham. With drink, sir?

Gui. No, my lord, with choler.

Ham. Your wisdom should show itself more richer to　300
　　signify this to the doctor; for, for me to put him
　　to his purgation would perhaps plunge him into
　　more choler.

Gui. Good my lord, put your discourse into some frame,
　　and start not so wildly from my affair.

Ham. I am tame, sir; pronounce.

Gui. The queen, your mother, in most great affliction of
　　spirit, hath sent me to you.

Ham. You are welcome.

Gui. Nay, good my lord, this courtesy is not of the right　310
　　breed.　If it shall please you to make me a whole-
　　some answer, I will do your mother's command-

ment : if not, your pardon and my return shall be
the end of business.

Ham. Sir, I cannot.

Gui. What, my lord ?

Ham. Make you a wholesome answer ; my wit's dis-
eas'd : but, sir, such answer as I can make, you shall
command, or rather, as you say, my mother : therefore
no more, but to the matter ; my mother, you say,— 320

Ros. Then thus she says ; your behaviour hath struck her
into amazement and admiration.

Ham. O wonderful son, that can so stonish a mother !
But is there no sequel at the heels of this mother's
admiration ?   Impart.

Ros. She desires to speak with you in her closet ere you
go to bed.

Ham. We shall obey, were she ten times our mother.
Have you any further trade with us ?

Ros. My lord, you once did love me.   330

Ham. And do still, by these pickers and stealers.

Ros. Good my lord, what is your cause of distemper ?
You do surely bar the door upon your own liberty,
if you deny your griefs to your friend.

Ham. Sir, I lack advancement.

Ros. How can that be, when you have the voice of the
king himself for your succession in Denmark ?

Ham. Ay, sir, but ' while the grass grows,'—the proverb
is something musty.

Re-enter Players with recorders

O, the recorders! let me see one. To withdraw 340
with you:—why do you go about to recover the
wind of me, as if you would drive me into a toil?

Gui. O, my lord, if my duty be too bold, my love is too
unmannerly.

Ham. I do not well understand that. Will you play
upon this pipe?

Gui. My lord, I cannot.

Ham. I pray you.

Gui. Believe me, I cannot.

Ham. I do beseech you. 350

Gui. I know no touch of it, my lord.

Ham. It is as easy as lying: govern these ventages with
your fingers and thumbs, give it breath with your †
mouth, and it will discourse most eloquent music;
look you, these are the stops.

Gui. But these cannot I command to any utterance of
harmony; I have not the skill.

Ham. Why, look you now how unworthy a thing you
make of me! You would play upon me, you would
seem to know my stops, you would pluck out the 360
heart of my mystery, you would sound me from my

lowest note to {the top of} my compass ; and there
is much music, excellent voice, in this little organ, yet
cannot you make it speak. 'Sblood, do you think
I am easier to be play'd on than a pipe ?   Call me
what instrument you will, though you can fret me,
yet you cannot play upon me.

Re-enter Polonius

God bless you, sir !

Pol. My lord, the queen would speak with you, and
presently.   370

Ham. Do you see yonder cloud that 's almost in shape of
a camel ?

Pol. By the mass and 'tis, like a camel indeed.

Ham. Methinks it is like a weasel.

Pol. It is back'd like a weasel.

Ham. Or like a whale.

Pol. Very like a whale.

Ham. Then I will come to my mother by and by.   (*aside*)
They fool me to the top of my bent.   I will come
by and by.   Leave me, friends.   I will, say so.   380

Exeunt all but Hamlet

'By and by' is easily said.
'Tis now the very witching time of night,
When churchyards yawn, and hell itself breaks out
Contagion to this world: now could I drink hot blood,

97

And do such bitter business as the day
Would quake to look on.   Soft ! now to my mother.
O heart, lose not thy nature, let not ever
The soul of Nero enter this firm bosom ;
Let me be cruel, not unnatural :
I will speak daggers to her, but use none ;   390
My tongue and soul in this be hypocrites ;
How in my words somever she be shent,
To give them seals never my soul consent !   *Exit*

SCENE III

A room in the castle

Enter King, Rosencrantz, and Guildenstern

Ki.   I like him not, nor stands it safe with us
To let his madness range.   Therefore prepare you ;
I your commission will forthwith dispatch,
And he to England shall along with you :
The terms of our estate may not endure
Hazard so near us as doth hourly grow
Out of his braves.   †

Gui.   We will ourselves provide :
Most holy and religious fear it is
To keep those many many bodies safe

98

That live and feed upon your majesty.   10

Ros. The single and peculiar life is bound
With all the strength and armour of the mind
To keep itself from noyance, but much more
That spirit upon whose weal depends and rests
The lives of many.   The cease of majesty
Dies not alone, but like a gulf doth draw
What's near it with it : or it is a massy wheel,
Fix'd on the summit of the highest mount,
To whose huge spokes ten thousand lesser things
Are mortis'd and adjoin'd, which when it falls,   20
Each small annexment, petty consequence,
Attends the boisterous ruin.   Never alone
Did the king sigh, but with a general groan.

Ki. Arm you, I pray you, to this speedy voyage,
For we will fetters put about this fear,
Which now goes too free-footed.

Ros. ⎫
Gui. ⎭   We will haste us.

Exeunt Rosencrantz and Guildenstern
Enter Polonius

Pol. My lord, he's going to his mother's closet :
Behind the arras I'll convey myself,
To hear the process : I'll warrant she'll tax him home :
And, as you said, and wisely was it said,   30

'Tis meet that some more audience than a mother,
Since nature makes them partial, should o'erhear
The speech of vantage.   Fare you well, my liege ;
I 'll call upon you ere you go to bed,
And tell you what I know.

Ki.   Thanks, dear my lord.

Exit Polonius

O, my offence is rank, it smells to heaven,
It hath the primal eldest curse upon 't,
A brother's murder.   Pray can I not ;
Though inclination be as sharp as will,
My stronger guilt defeats my strong intent,   40
And like a man to double business bound,
I stand in pause where I shall first begin,
And both neglect.   What if this cursed hand
Were thicker than itself with brother's blood,
Is there not rain enough in the sweet heavens
To wash it white as snow ?   Whereto serves mercy
But to confront the visage of offence ?
And what 's in prayer but this twofold force,
To be forestalled ere we come to fall,
Or pardon'd being down ?   Then I 'll look up ;   50
My fault is past.   But O, what form of prayer
Can serve my turn ?   ' Forgive me my foul murder ? '
That cannot be, since I am still possess'd

Of those effects for which I did the murder,
My crown, mine own ambition and my queen.
May one be pardon'd and retain the offence?
In the corrupted currents of this world
Offence's gilded hand may shove by justice,
And oft 'tis seen the wicked prize itself
Buys out the law: but 'tis not so above;   60
There is no shuffling, there the action lies
In his true nature, and we ourselves compell'd
Even to the teeth and forehead of our faults
To give in evidence.   What then? what rests?
Try what repentance can: what can it not?
Yet what can it when one can not repent?
O wretched state!   O bosom black as death!
O limed soul, that struggling to be free
Art more engag'd!   Help, angels! make assay!
Bow, stubborn knees, and, heart with strings of steel,   70
Be soft as sinews of the new-born babe!
All may be well.   *Retires and kneels*

Enter Hamlet

Ham. Now might I do it, but now 'a is a-praying;
And now I'll do it, and so he goes to heaven,
And so am I reveng'd?   That would be scann'd;
A villain kills my father, and for that,
I, his sole son, do this same villain send

I   101

    To heaven.

    Why, this is hire and salary, not revenge.   ✝

    'A took my father grossly, full of bread,   80

    With all his crimes broad blown, as flush as May;

    And how his audit stands who knows save heaven?

    But in our circumstance and course of thought,

    'Tis heavy with him: and am I then reveng'd,

    To take him in the purging of his soul,

    When he is fit and season'd for his passage?

    No.

    Up, sword, and know thou a more horrid hent,

    When he is drunk, asleep, or in his rage,

    Or in the incestuous pleasure of his bed,   90

    At game, a-swearing, or about some act

    That has no relish of salvation in't,

    Then trip him, that his heels may kick at heaven,

    And that his soul may be as damn'd and black

    As hell whereto it goes.   My mother stays:

    This physic but prolongs thy sickly days.   *Exit*

Ki. (*rising*) My words fly up, my thoughts remain below:

    Words without thoughts never to heaven go. *Exit*

SCENE IV

The Queen's closet

Enter Queen and Polonius

arras c.

Pol. 'A will come straight; look you lay home to him,
Tell him his pranks have been too broad to bear with,
And that your grace hath screen'd and stood between
Much heat and him.   I'll silence me even here.
Pray you, be round {with him.

Ham.   (*within*) Mother, mother, mother!}

Qu.   I'll warrant you; fear me not.
Withdraw, I hear him coming.

                    Polonius hides behind the arras ✓

Enter Hamlet

Ham. Now, mother, what's the matter?

Qu. Hamlet, thou hast thy father much offended.

Ham. Mother, you have my father much offended.   10

Qu. Come, come, you answer with an idle tongue.

Ham. Go, go, you question with a wicked tongue.

Qu. Why, how now, Hamlet?

Ham.   What's the matter now?

Qu. Have you forgot me?

Ham.   No, by the rood, not so:
You are the queen, your husband's brother's wife,

And would it were not so, you are my mother.

Qu. Nay, then, I'll set those to you that can speak.

Ham. Come, come, and sit you down; you shall not budge;
You go not till I set you up a glass
Where you may see the inmost part of you.   20

Qu. What wilt thou do? thou wilt not murder me?
Help, ho!

Pol. (*behind*) What, ho! help, {help, help!}

Ham. (*drawing*) How now! a rat?   Dead for a ducat,
dead!   *Makes a pass through the arras*

Pol. (*behind*) O, I am slain!

Qu.   O me, what hast thou done?

Ham. Nay, I know not, is it the king?

Qu. O, what a rash and bloody deed is this!

Ham. A bloody deed; almost as bad, good mother,
As kill a king, and marry with his brother.

Qu. As kill a king?

Ham.   Ay, lady, it was my word.   30

Lifts up the arras and discovers Polonius

Thou wretched, rash, intruding fool, farewell;
I took thee for thy better; take thy fortune;
Thou find'st to be too busy is some danger.
Leave wringing of your hands: peace! sit you down,
And let me wring your heart, for so I shall,
If it be made of penetrable stuff,

If damned custom have not brass'd it so,
That it be proof and bulwark against sense.

Qu. What have I done, that thou dar'st wag thy tongue
In noise so rude against me?

Ham.   Such an act   40
That blurs the grace and blush of modesty,
Calls virtue hypocrite, takes off the rose
From the fair forehead of an innocent love,
And sets a blister there, makes marriage vows
As false as dicers' oaths, O, such a deed
As from the body of contraction plucks
The very soul, and sweet religion makes
A rhapsody of words : heaven's face does glow   †
O'er this solidity and compound mass,
With heated visage, as against the doom   50
Is thought-sick at the act.

Qu.   Ay me, what act,
That roars so loud and thunders in the index?

Ham. Look here, upon this picture, and on this,
The counterfeit presentment of two brothers.
See what a grace was seated on this brow ;
Hyperion's curls, the front of Jove himself,
An eye like Mars, to threaten and command,
A station like the herald Mercury
New-lighted on a heaven-kissing hill ;

A combination and a form indeed,   60
Where every god did seem to set his seal
To give the world assurance of a man :
This was your husband.   Look you now what follows :
Here is your husband, like a mildew'd ear,
Blasting his wholesome brother.   Have you eyes ?
Could you on this fair mountain leave to feed,
And batten on this moor ?   Ha ! have you eyes ?
You cannot call it love, for at your age
The hey-day in the blood is tame, it's humble,
And waits upon the judgement, and what judgement 70
Would step from this to this ?   [Sense sure you have,
Else could you not have motion, but sure that sense
Is apoplex'd, for madness would not err,
Nor sense to ecstasy was ne'er so thrall'd
But it reserv'd some quantity of choice,
To serve in such a difference.]   What devil was 't
That thus hath cozen'd you at hoodman-blind ?
[Eyes without feeling, feeling without sight,
Ears without hands or eyes, smelling sans all,
Or but a sickly part of one true sense   80
Could not so mope.]   O shame ! where is thy blush ?
Rebellious hell,
If thou canst mutine in a matron's bones,
To flaming youth let virtue be as wax

And melt in her own fire ; proclaim no shame
When the compulsive ardour gives the charge,
Since frost itself as actively doth burn,
And reason pandars will.

Qu.   O Hamlet, speak no more :
Thou turn'st my very eyes into my soul,
And there I see such black and grained spots   90
As will leave there their tint.

Ham.   Nay, but to live
In the rank sweat of an enseamed bed,
Stew'd in corruption, honeying and making love
Over the nasty sty,—

Qu.   O, speak to me no more ;
These words like daggers enter in my ears ;
No more, sweet Hamlet !

Ham.   A murderer and a villain,
A slave that is not twentieth part the tithe
Of your precedent lord, a Vice of kings,
A cutpurse of the empire and the rule,
That from a shelf the precious diadem stole   100
And put it in his pocket !

Qu.   No more !

Ham. A king of shreds and patches—

Enter Ghost

Save me and hover o'er me with your wings,

    You heavenly guards! What would your gracious
        figure?

Qu. Alas, he 's mad!

Ham. Do you not come your tardy son to chide,
    That, laps'd in time and passion, lets go by
    The important acting of your dread command?
    O, say!

Gho. Do not forget: this visitation   110
    Is but to whet thy almost blunted purpose.
    But look, amazement on thy mother sits;
    O, step between her and her fighting soul:
    Conceit in weakest bodies strongest works,
    Speak to her, Hamlet.

Ham.   How is it with you, lady?

Qu. Alas, how is 't with you,
    That you do bend your eye on vacancy,
    And with the incorporal air do hold discourse?
    Forth at your eyes your spirits wildly peep,
    And, as the sleeping soldiers in the alarm,   120
    Your bedded hair, like life in excrements,
    Start up and stand an end. O gentle son,
    Upon the heat and flame of thy distemper
    Sprinkle cool patience. Whereon do you look?

Ham. On him, on him. Look you how pale he glares!
    His form and cause conjoin'd, preaching to stones,

Would make them capable.   Do not look upon me,
Lest with this piteous action you convert
My stern effects : then what I have to do
Will want true colour ; tears perchance for blood.   130

Qu. To whom do you speak this ?

Ham.   Do you see nothing there ?

Qu. Nothing at all ; yet all that is I see.

Ham. Nor did you nothing hear ?

Qu.   No, nothing but ourselves.

Ham. Why, look you there ! look, how it steals away !
My father, in his habit as he liv'd !
Look, where he goes, even now out at the portal !

                                        Exit Ghost

Qu. This is the very coinage of your brain :
This bodiless creation ecstasy
Is very cunning in.

Ham.   {Ecstasy !}
My pulse, as yours, doth temperately keep time,   140
And makes as healthful music : it is not madness
That I have utter'd ; bring me to the test,
And I the matter will re-word, which madness
Would gambol from.   Mother, for love of grace,
Lay not that flattering unction to your soul,
That not your trespass but my madness speaks,
It will but skin and film the ulcerous place,

Whiles rank corruption, mining all within,
Infects unseen.   Confess yourself to heaven,
Repent what's past, avoid what is to come,   15●
And do not spread the compost on the weeds
To make them ranker.   Forgive me this my virtue:
For in the fatness of these pursy times
Virtue itself of vice must pardon beg,
Yea, curb and woo for leave to do him good.
Qu. O Hamlet, thou hast cleft my heart in twain.
Ham. O, throw away the worser part of it,
And live the purer with the other half.
Good night: but go not to my uncle's bed;
Assume a virtue, if you have it not.   16●
[That monster, custom, who all sense doth eat,   †
Of habits devil, is angel yet in this,
That to the use of actions fair and good
He likewise gives a frock or livery,
That aptly is put on.]   Refrain to-night,
And that shall lend a kind of easiness
To the next abstinence; [the next more easy;
For use almost can change the stamp of nature,
And either . . . the devil, or throw him out
With wondrous potency.]   Once more, good
       night: 17
And when you are desirous to be blest,

I 'll blessing beg of you.   For this same lord,

Pointing to Polonius

I do repent : but heaven hath pleas'd it so
To punish me with this, and this with me,
That I must be their scourge and minister.
I will bestow him, and will answer well
The death I gave him.   So, again, good night ;
I must be cruel, only to be kind :
This bad begins, and worse remains behind.
[One word more, good lady.]

Qu.   What shall I do ?   180

Ham. Not this, by no means, that I bid you do :
Let the blowt king tempt you again to bed,
Pinch wanton on your cheek, call you his mouse,
And let him, for a pair of reechy kisses,
Or paddling in your neck with his damn'd fingers,
Make you to ravel all this matter out,
That I essentially am not in madness,
But mad in craft ; 'twere good you let him know ;
For who, that 's but a queen, fair, sober, wise,
Would from a paddock, from a bat, a gib,   190
Such dear concernings hide ! who would do so ?
No, in despite of sense and secrecy,
Unpeg the basket on the house's top,
Let the birds fly, and like the famous ape,   †

111

To try conclusions, in the basket creep
And break your own neck down.

Qu. Be thou assur'd, if words be made of breath
And breath of life, I have no life to breathe
What thou hast said to me.

Ham. I must to England ; you know that ?

Qu.   Alack,   200
I had forgot : 'tis so concluded on.

Ham. [There's letters seal'd : and my two schoolfellows,
Whom I will trust as I will adders fang'd,
They bear the mandate ; they must sweep my way,
And marshal me to knavery.   Let it work ;
For 'tis the sport to have the enginer
Hoist with his own petar, and 't shall go hard
But I will delve one yard below their mines,
And blow them at the moon : O, 'tis most sweet
When in one line two crafts directly meet.]   210
This man shall set me packing :
I 'll lug the guts into the neighbour room.
Mother, good night indeed : this counsellor
Is now most still, most secret, and most grave,
Who was in life a most foolish prating knave.
Come, sir, to draw toward an end with you.
Good night, mother.

                 Exeunt severally ; Hamlet dragging in Polonius

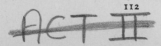

Act Fourth

SCENE I

A room in the castle

Enter King, Queen, Rosencrantz, and Guildenstern

Ki. There's matter in these sighs, these profound heaves ;
You must translate, 'tis fit we understand them.
Where is your son ?

Qu. [Bestow this place on us a little while.]

        Exeunt Rosencrantz and Guildenstern

Ah, mine own lord, what have I seen to-night !

Ki. What, Gertrude ?   How does Hamlet ?

Qu. Mad as the sea and wind when both contend
Which is the mightier, in his lawless fit,
Behind the arras hearing something stir,
Whips out his rapier, cries ' A rat, a rat ! '   **10**
And in this brainish apprehension kills
The unseen good old man.

Ki.   O heavy deed !
It had been so with us, had we been there ;
His liberty is full of threats to all,
To you yourself, to us, to every one ;

Alas, how shall this bloody deed be answer'd?
It will be laid to us, whose providence
Should have kept short, restrain'd, and out of haunt,
This mad young man : but so much was our love,   20
We would not understand what was most fit,
But, like the owner of a foul disease,
To keep it from divulging, let it feed
Even on the pith of life.   Where is he gone?

Qu. To draw apart the body he hath kill'd :
O'er whom his very madness, like some ore
Among a mineral of metals base,
Shows itself pure ; 'a weeps for what is done.

Ki. O Gertrude, come away!
The sun no sooner shall the mountains touch,
But we will ship him hence : and this vile deed   30
We must, with all our majesty and skill,
Both countenance and excuse.   Ho, Guildenstern!

Re-enter Rosencrantz and Guildenstern

Friends both, go join you with some further aid ;
Hamlet in madness hath Polonius slain,
And from his mother's closet hath he dragg'd him :
Go seek him out, speak fair, and bring the body
Into the chapel.   I pray you, haste in this.

Exeunt Rosencrantz and Guildenstern

Come, Gertrude, we'll call up our wisest friends,

And let them know both what we mean to do
And what 's untimely done.   40
[Whose whisper o'er the world's diameter
As level as the cannon to his blank
Transports his poison'd shot, may miss our name
And hit the woundless air.]   O, come away !
My soul is full of discord and dismay.   *Exeunt*

SCENE II

Another room in the castle

Enter Hamlet

Ham. Safely stow'd.

Ros. } *(within)* Hamlet ! Lord Hamlet.}
Gui.

Ham. [But soft,] what noise ? who calls on Hamlet ?
    O, here they come.

Enter Rosencrantz and Guildenstern

Ros. What have you done, my lord, with the dead body ?

Ham. Compounded it with dust, whereto 'tis kin.

Ros. Tell us where 'tis, that we may take it thence,
    And bear it to the chapel.

Ham. Do not believe it.

Ros. Believe what ?   10

115

Ham. That I can keep your counsel and not mine own. Besides, to be demanded of a sponge, what replication should be made by the son of a king?

Ros. Take you me for a sponge, my lord?

Ham. Ay, sir; that soaks up the king's countenance, his rewards, his authorities. But such officers do the king best service in the end: he keeps them, like an ape, in the corner of his jaw, first mouth'd, to † be last swallow'd: when he needs what you have glean'd, it is but squeezing you, and, sponge, you 2 shall be dry again.

Ros. I understand you not, my lord.

Ham. I am glad of it: a knavish speech sleeps in a foolish ear.

Ros. My lord, you must tell us where the body is, and go with us to the king.

Ham. The body is with the king, but the king is not with the body. The king is a thing—

Gui. A thing, my lord?

Ham. Of nothing: bring me to him. {Hide fox, and 3 all after.} *Exeunt*

SCENE III

Another room in the castle

Enter King, attended

Ki. I have sent to seek him, and to find the body.
How dangerous is it that this man goes loose !
Yet must not we put the strong law on him ;
He 's loved of the distracted multitude,
Who like not in their judgement, but their eyes ;
And where 'tis so, the offender's scourge is weigh'd,
But never the offence. To bear all smooth and
        even,
This sudden sending him away must seem
Deliberate pause : diseases desperate grown
By desperate appliance are reliev'd,   10
Or not at all.

Enter Rosencrantz and others

    How now ! what hath befall'n ?

Ros. Where the dead body is bestow'd, my lord,
We cannot get from him.

Ki.   But where is he ?

Ros. Without, my lord, guarded to know your pleasure.

Ki. Bring him before us.

Ros. Ho, bring in the lord.

 K

Enter Hamlet guarded

Ki. Now, Hamlet, where's Polonius?

Ham. At supper.

Ki. At supper, where?

Ham. Not where he eats, but where he is eaten: a certain   20
convocation of politic worms are e'en at him. Your
worm is your only emperor for diet: we fat all creatures else to fat us, and we fat ourselves for maggots:
your fat king and your lean beggar is but variable
service, two dishes, but to one table: that's the end.

[*Ki.* Alas, alas!

Ham. A man may fish with the worm that hath eat of a
king, and eat of the fish that hath fed of that worm.]

Ki. What dost thou mean by this?

Ham. Nothing but to show you how a king may go a   30
progress through the guts of a beggar.

Ki. Where is Polonius?

Ham. In heaven; send thither to see: if your messenger
find him not there, seek him i' the other place
yourself; but if indeed you find him not within
this month, you shall nose him as you go up the
stairs into the lobby.

Ki. Go seek him there.   *To some Attendants*

Ham. 'A will stay till you come.   *Exeunt Attendants*

Ki. Hamlet, this deed, for thine especial safety,   40

Which we do tender, as we dearly grieve
For that which thou hast done, must send thee hence
{With fiery quickness} : therefore prepare thyself ;
The bark is ready, and the wind at help,
The associates tend, and every thing is bent
For England.

Ham.　　　　　For England ?

Ki.　　　　　　　　　Ay, Hamlet.

Ham.　　　　　　　　　　　Good.

Ki. So is it, if thou knew'st our purposes.

Ham. I see a cherub that sees them.   But, come, for
　　England !   Farewell, dear mother.

Ki. Thy loving father, Hamlet.　　　　　　　　　50

Ham. My mother ; father and mother is man and wife,
　　man and wife is one flesh, so my mother.   Come,
　　for England !　　　　　　　　　　　　*Exit*

Ki. Follow him at foot, tempt him with speed aboard,
　　Delay it not ; I 'll have him hence to-night :
　　Away ! for every thing is seal'd and done
　　That else leans on the affair : pray you, make haste ;
　　　　　　　Exeunt Rosencrantz and Guildenstern
　　And, England, if my love thou hold'st at aught—
　　As my great power thereof may give thee sense,
　　Since yet thy cicatrice looks raw and red　　　　60
　　After the Danish sword ; and thy free awe

Pays homage to us, thou mayst not coldly set
Our sovereign process, which imports at full,
By letters congruing to that effect,
The present death of Hamlet.   Do it, England ;
For like the hectic in my blood he rages,
And thou must cure me : till I know 'tis done,
Howe'er my haps, my joys will ne'er begin.   *Exit* †

SCENE IV

The next day

A plain in Denmark

Enter Fortinbras with his army over the stage

For. Go, captain, from me greet the Danish king ;
Tell him that by his licence Fortinbras
Craves the conveyance of a promis'd march
Over his kingdom.   You know the rendezvous.
If that his majesty would aught with us,
We shall express our duty in his eye ;
And let him know so.

Cap.   I will do 't, my lord.

For. Go softly on.   *Exeunt* [*Fortinbras and Soldiers*
          Enter Hamlet, Rosencrantz, Guildenstern, and others

Ham. Good sir, whose powers are these ?

Cap. They are of Norway, sir.   10

Ham. How purpos'd, sir, I pray you ?

Cap. Against some part of Poland.

Ham. Who commands them, sir ?

Cap. The nephew to old Norway, Fortinbras.

Ham. Goes it against the main of Poland, sir,
    Or for some frontier ?

Cap. Truly to speak, and with no addition,
    We go to gain a little patch of ground
    That hath in it no profit but the name.
    To pay five ducats, five, I would not farm it ;   20
    Nor will it yield to Norway or the Pole
    A ranker rate, should it be sold in fee.

Ham. Why then the Polack never will defend it.

Cap. Yes, it is already garrison'd.

Ham. Two thousand souls and twenty thousand ducats
    Will not debate the question of this straw :   †
    This is the imposthume of much wealth and peace,
    That inward breaks, and shows no cause without
    Why the man dies.   I humbly thank you, sir.

Cap. God be wi' you, sir.   *Exit*

Ros.   Will 't please you go, my lord ?   30

Ham. I 'll be with you straight, go a little before.

                   Exeunt all but Hamlet

    How all occasions do inform against me,

And spur my dull revenge !   What is a man,
If his chief good and market of his time
Be but to sleep and feed ? a beast, no more.
Sure, he that made us with such large discourse,
Looking before and after, gave us not
That capability and god-like reason
To fust in us unus'd.   Now, whether it be
Bestial oblivion, or some craven scruple   40
Of thinking too precisely on the event,—
A thought which, quarter'd, hath but one part wisdom
And ever three parts coward,—I do not know
Why yet I live to say ' this thing 's to do,'
Sith I have cause, and will, and strength, and means
To do 't.   Examples gross as earth exhort me ;
Witness this army of such mass and charge,
Led by a delicate and tender prince,
Whose spirit with divine ambition puff'd
Makes mouths at the invisible event,   50
Exposing what is mortal and unsure
To all that fortune, death, and danger dare,
Even for an egg-shell.   Rightly to be great
Is not to stir without great argument,   †
But greatly to find quarrel in a straw
When honour 's at the stake.   How stand I then,
That have a father kill'd, a mother stain'd,

Excitements of my reason and my blood,
And let all sleep, while to my shame I see
The imminent death of twenty thousand men, 60
That for a fantasy and trick of fame
Go to their graves like beds, fight for a plot
Whereon the numbers cannot try the cause,
Which is not tomb enough and continent
To hide the slain ?   O, from this time forth,
My thoughts be bloody, or be nothing worth !

ACT II *Exit*]

SCENE V

A few days later

Elsinore.   A room in the castle

Enter Queen, Horatio, [and a Gentleman] †

Qu. I will not speak with her.
Gen. She is importunate, indeed distract :
Her mood will needs be pitied.

Qu.   What would she have ?
Gen. She speaks much of her father, says she hears
There 's tricks i' the world, and hems and beats her heart,
Spurns enviously at straws, speaks things in doubt,
That carry but half sense : her speech is nothing,
Yet the unshaped use of it doth move

The hearers to collection ; they aim at it,
And botch the words up fit to their own thoughts ;   10
Which, as her winks, and nods, and gestures yield them,
Indeed would make one think there might be thought,
Though nothing sure, yet much unhappily.

Hor. 'Twere good she were spoken with, for she may strew
Dangerous conjectures in ill-breeding minds.
Let her come in.   *Exit Gentleman*

Qu. (*aside*) To my sick soul, as sin's true nature is,
Each toy seems prologue to some great amiss :
So full of artless jealousy is guilt,
It spills itself in fearing to be spilt.   20

Enter Ophelia

Oph. Where is the beauteous majesty of Denmark ?

Qu. How now, Ophelia ?

Oph. (*sings*) How should I your true love know
              From another one ?
          By his cockle hat and staff
              And his sandal shoon.

Qu. Alas, sweet lady, what imports this song ?

Oph. Say you ? nay, pray you, mark.
      (*sings*) He is dead and gone, lady,
              He is dead and gone,   30
          At his head a grass-green turf,
              At his heels a stone.

O ho!

Qu.　　　Nay, but Ophelia,—

Oph.　　　　　　　Pray you, mark.

　　(*sings*) White his shroud as the mountain snow,—

　　　　　　　　Enter King

Qu. Alas, look here, my lord.

Oph. (*sings*)　　Larded all with sweet flowers ;

　　　　　　Which bewept to the grave did not go

　　　　　　　　With true-love showers.

Ki. How do you, pretty lady ?

Oph. Well, God 'ild you !　They say the owl was a baker's　40
　　daughter ; Lord, we know what we are, but know
　　not what we may be.　God be at your table !

Ki. Conceit upon her father.

Oph. Pray, let 's have no words of this, but when they
　　ask you what it means, say you this :

　　(*sings*) To-morrow is Saint Valentine's day,

　　　　　　　All in the morning betime,

　　　　　And I a maid at your window,

　　　　　　　To be your Valentine.

　　　　　Then up he rose, and donn'd his clo'es,　　50

　　　　　　　And dupp'd the chamber-door,

　　　　　Let in the maid, that out a maid

　　　　　　　Never departed more.

i. Pretty Ophelia !

Oph. Indeed, without an oath, I 'll make an end on 't :

(*sings*) By Gis and by Saint Charity,
    Alack, and fie for shame !
    Young men will do 't, if they come to 't,
      By cock, they are to blame.
    Quoth she, before you tumbled me,   60
      You promised me to wed.

He answers :

    So would I ha' done, by yonder sun,
      An thou hadst not come to my bed.

Ki. How long hath she been thus ?

Oph. I hope all will be well, we must be patient, but I
cannot choose but weep to think they would lay
him i' the cold ground, my brother shall know
of it, and so I thank you for your good counsel.
Come, my coach ! Good night, ladies, good   70
night ; sweet ladies, good night, good night. *Exit*

Ki. Follow her close, give her good watch, I pray you.

                     Exit Horatio

O, this is the poison of deep grief ; it springs
All from her father's death, and now behold !
O Gertrude, Gertrude,
When sorrows come, they come not single spies,
But in battalions. First, her father slain ;
Next, your son gone, and he most violent author

6

Of his own just remove ; the people muddied,
Thick and unwholesome in their thoughts, and
    whispers   80
For good Polonius' death : and we have done but
    greenly,
In hugger-mugger to inter him : poor Ophelia
Divided from herself, and her fair judgement,
Without the which we are pictures, or mere beasts ;
Last, and as much containing as all these,
Her brother is in secret come from France,
Feeds on this wonder, keeps himself in clouds,
And wants not buzzers to infect his ear
With pestilent speeches of his father's death ;
Wherein necessity, of matter beggar'd,   90
Will nothing stick our person to arraign
In ear and ear.   O my dear Gertrude, this,
Like to a murdering-piece, in many places
Gives me superfluous death.   *A noise within*

Qu.   Alack, what noise is this ?

Ki. Attend, where are my Switzers ? Let them guard
    the door.

            Enter a Messenger

What is the matter ?

Mes.   Save yourself, my lord :
The ocean, overpeering of his list,

Eats not the flats with more impiteous haste

The ~~Than~~ young Laertes in a riotous head

O'erbears your officers : the rabble call him lord ;   10

~~And, as the world were now but to begin,~~

~~Antiquity forgot, custom not known,~~

The ratifiers and props of every word,

They cry ' Choose we ; Laertes shall be king ! '

Caps, hands and tongues applaud it to the clouds,

' Laertes shall be king, Laertes king ! '

Qu. How cheerfully on the false trail they cry !

Noise within

O, this is counter, you false Danish dogs !

Ki. ~~The doors are broke.~~

Enter Laertes, armed ; Danes following

Lae. Where is this king ? Sirs, stand you all without. 11

Danes. No, let's come in.

Lae.   I pray you, give me leave.

Danes. We will, we will.   *They retire without the door*

Lae. I thank you : keep the door. O thou vile king,

Give me my father !

Qu.   Calmly, good Laertes.

Lae. That drop of blood that's calm proclaims me bastard,

Cries cuckold to my father, brands the harlot

Even here, between the chaste unsmirched brow

Of my true mother.

Ki.   What is the cause, Laertes,
That thy rebellion looks so giant-like ?
Let him go, Gertrude ; do not fear our person :   120
There 's such divinity doth hedge a king,
That treason can but peep to what it would,
Acts little of his will.   Tell me, Laertes,
Why thou art thus incens'd : let him go, Gertrude :
Speak, man.

Lae. Where is my father ?

Ki.   Dead.

Qu.   But not by him.

Ki. Let him demand his fill.

Lae. How came he dead ?   I 'll not be juggled with :
To hell, allegiance ! vows, to the blackest devil !
Conscience and grace, to the profoundest pit !   130
I dare damnation : to this point I stand,
That both the worlds I give to negligence,
Let come what comes ; only I 'll be reveng'd
Most throughly for my father.

Ki.   Who shall stay you ?

Lae. My will, not all the world 's :
And for my means, I 'll husband them so well,
They shall go far with little.

Ki.   Good Laertes,
If you desire to know the certainty

Of your dear father, is 't writ in your revenge
That, swoopstake, you will draw both friend and foe,
Winner and loser?   14]

Lae. None but his enemies.

Ki.   Will you know them then?

Lae. To his good friends thus wide I 'll ope my arms;
And, like the kind life-rendering pelican,
Repast them with my blood.

Ki.   Why, now you speak
Like a good child and a true gentleman.
That I am guiltless of your father's death,
And am most sensibly in grief for it,
It shall as level to your judgement 'pear
As day does to your eye.

Danes (*within*)   Let her come in.   15(

Lae. How now, what noise is that?

Re-enter Ophelia

O heat, dry up my brains! tears seven times salt,
Burn out the sense and virtue of mine eye!
By heaven, thy madness shall be paid with weight,
Till our scale turn the beam.   O rose of May,
Dear maid, kind sister, sweet Ophelia!
O heavens! is 't possible a young maid's wits
Should be as mortal as an old man's life?   †
{Nature is fine in love, and where 'tis fine

It sends some precious instançe of itself   160
After the thing it loves.}

Oph. (*sings*) They bore him barefac'd on the bier :
{Hey non nonny, nonny, hey nonney :}
And in his grave rain'd many a tear,—
Fare you well, my dove !

Lae. Hadst thou thy wits, and didst persuade revenge,
It could not move thus.

Oph. (*sings*) You must sing a-down a-down,
An you call him a-down-a.

O, how the wheel becomes it ! It is the false 17c
steward that stole his master's daughter.

Lae. This nothing's more than matter.

Oph. There's rosemary, that's for remembrance ; pray
you, love, remember ; and there is pansies, that's
for thoughts.

Lae. A document in madness, thoughts and remembrance fitted.

Oph. There's fennel for you, and columbines, there's
rue for you, and here's some for me, we may call
it herb of grace o' Sundays, you may wear your 180
rue with a difference, there's a daisy, I would give
you some violets, but they wither'd all when my
father died, they say 'a made a good end,—
(*sings*) For bonnie sweet Robin is all my joy.

Lae. Thought and afflictions, passion, hell itself,
  She turns to favour and to prettiness.

Oph. (*sings*) And will 'a not come again ?
    And will 'a not come again ?
     No, no, he is dead,
     Go to thy death-bed,   190
    He never will come again.

    His beard was as white as snow,
    Flaxen was his poll :
     He is gone, he is gone,
     And we cast away moan,
    God ha' mercy on his soul !
  And of all Christian souls, {I pray God.}   God be
  wi' you.   *Exit*

Lae. Do you see this, O God ?

Ki. Laertes, I must commune with your grief,
  Or you deny me right.   Go but apart,   200
  Make choice of whom your wisest friends you will,
  And they shall hear and judge 'twixt you and me ;
  If by direct or by collateral hand
  They find us touch'd, we will our kingdom give,
  Our crown, our life, and all that we call ours,
  To you in satisfaction ; but if not,
  Be you content to lend your patience to us,
  And we shall jointly labour with your soul

To give it due content.

Lae.   Let this be so.

His means of death, his obscure funeral,   210
No trophy, sword, nor hatchment o'er his bones,
No noble rite, nor formal ostentation,
Cry to be heard, as 'twere from heaven to earth,
That I must call 't in question.

Ki.   So you shall ;
And where the offence is, let the great axe fall.
I pray you, go with me.   *Exeunt*

SCENE VI

Another room in the castle

Enter Horatio and a Servant

Hor. What are they that would speak with me ?
Ser. Sea-faring men, sir : they say they have letters for you.
Hor. Let them come in.   *Exit Servant*
    I do not know from what part of the world
    I should be greeted ; if not from Lord Hamlet.

Enter Sailors

First Sail. God bless you, sir.
Hor. Let him bless thee too.
First Sail. 'A shall, sir, an please him.   There's a letter

L   133

for you, sir, it came from the ambassador that was
bound for England, if your name be Horatio, as I am   10
let to know it is.

Hor. (*reads*) 'Horatio, when thou shalt have overlook'd
this, give these fellows some means to the king : they
have letters for him. Ere we were two days old
at sea, a pirate of very warlike appointment gave us
chase ; finding ourselves too slow of sail, we put on
a compell'd valour, and in the grapple I boarded
them, on the instant they got clear of our ship, so I
alone became their prisoner. They have dealt with
me like thieves of mercy, but they knew what they   20
did ; I am to do a turn for them. Let the king have
the letters I have sent, and repair thou to me with as
much speed as thou wouldest fly death ; I have words
to speak in thine ear will make thee dumb, yet are
they much too light for the bore of the matter. These
good fellows will bring thee where I am. Rosencrantz and Guildenstern hold their course for
England : of them I have much to tell thee. Farewell.   'He that thou knowest thine HAMLET.

Come, I will give you way for these your letters
And do 't the speedier, that you may direct me
To him from whom you brought them.   *Exeunt*

SCENE VII

Another room in the castle

to P 133

Enter King and Laertes

Ki. Now must your conscience my acquittance seal,
And you must put me in your heart for friend,
Sith you have heard, and with a knowing ear,
That he which hath your noble father slain
Pursued my life.

Lae.   It well appears : but tell me
Why you proceeded not against these feats,
So criminal and so capital in nature,
As by your safety, wisdom, all things else,
You mainly were stirr'd up.

Ki.   O, for two special reasons,
Which may to you perhaps seem much unsinew'd,   10
But yet to me they 're strong. The queen his mother
Lives almost by his looks ; and for myself—
My virtue or my plague, be it either which—
She 's so conjunctive to my life and soul,
That, as the star moves not but in his sphere,
I could not but by her. The other motive,
Why to a public count I might not go,
Is the great love the general gender bear him ;

Who, dipping all his faults in their affection,
Work, like the spring that turneth wood to stone,   20
Convert his gyves to graces, so that my arrows,
Too slightly timber'd for so loud a wind,
Would have reverted to my bow again
But not where I have aim'd them.

Lae. And so have I a noble father lost ;
A sister driven into desperate terms,
Whose worth, if praises may go back again,
Stood challenger on mount of all the age
For her perfections : but my revenge will come.

Ki. Break not your sleeps for that : you must not think   30
That we are made of stuff so flat and dull
That we can let our beard be shook with danger,
And think it pastime.   You shortly shall hear more :
I lov'd your father, and we love ourself ;
And that, I hope, will teach you to imagine—

           Enter a Messenger, with letters

{How now ! what news ?

Mes.   Letters, my lord, from Hamlet :}
These to your majesty ; this to the queen.

Ki. From Hamlet ? who brought them ?

Mes. Sailors, my lord, they say ; I saw them not :
They were given me by Claudio ; he receiv'd them   40
Of him that brought them.

Ki.   Laertes, you shall hear them.
Leave us.   *Exit Messenger*
(*reads*) 'High and mighty, you shall know I am set
naked on your kingdom.   To-morrow shall I beg
leave to see your kingly eyes, when I shall, first asking
you pardon, thereunto recount the occasion of my
sudden {and more strange} return.

{' HAMLET.'}

What should this mean ?   Are all the rest come back ?
Or is it some abuse, and no such thing ?
Lae. Know you the hand ?   50
Ki. 'Tis Hamlet's character.   'Naked' !
And in a postscript here, he says 'alone':
Can you devise me ?
Lae. I am lost in it, my lord.   But let him come ;
It warms the very sickness in my heart,
That I shall live and tell him to his teeth,
' Thus didst thou.'
Ki.   If it be so, Laertes,—
As how should it be so ?   how otherwise ?—
Will you be ruled by me ?
Lae.   [Ay, my lord ;]
So you will not o'errule me to a peace.   60
Ki. To thine own peace.   If he be now return'd,

As checking at his voyage, and that he means
~~No more to undertake it,~~ I will work him
To an exploit now ripe in my device,
Under the which he shall not choose but fall :
And for his death no wind of blame shall breathe,
But even his mother shall uncharge the practice,
And call it accident.

[*Lae.*   My lord, I will be rul'd;   †
The rather, if you could devise it so
That I might be the organ.

Ki.   It falls right. 70
You have been talk'd of since your travel much,
And that in Hamlet's hearing, for a quality
Wherein they say you shine : your sum of parts
Did not together pluck such envy from him,
As did that one, and that in my regard
Of the unworthiest siege.

Lae.   What part is that, my lord ?

Ki. A very riband in the cap of youth,
Yet needful too ; for youth no less becomes
The light and careless livery that it wears
Than settled age his sables and his weeds, 80
Importing health and graveness.] Two months since,
Here was a gentleman of Normandy :—
I've seen myself, and serv'd against, the French,

138

And they can well on horseback: but this gallant
Had witchcraft in 't; he grew unto his seat,
And to such wondrous doing brought his horse
As had he been incorps'd, and demi-natur'd
With the brave beast: so far he topp'd my thought
That I, in forgery of shapes and tricks,
Come short of what he did.

Lae.   A Norman was 't?   90

Ki. A Norman.

Lae. Upon my life, Lamond.

Ki.   The very same.

Lae. I know him well: he is the brooch indeed
And gem of all the nation.

Ki. He made confession of you,
And gave you such a masterly report
For art and exercise in your defence,
And for your rapier most especial,
That he cried out, 'twould be a sight indeed
If one could match you: [the scrimers of their nation,
He swore, had neither motion, guard, nor eye,   101
If you oppos'd them.]   Sir, this report of his
Did Hamlet so envenom with his envy
That he could nothing do but wish and beg
Your sudden coming o'er, to play with you.
Now, out of this—

Lae.   What out of this, my lord ?

Ki. Laertes, was your father dear to you ?
   Or are you like the painting of a sorrow,
   A face without a heart ?

Lae.   Why ask you this ?

Ki. Not that I think you did not love your father,   110
   But that I know love is begun by time,
   And that I see, in passages of proof,
   Time qualifies the spark and fire of it.
   [There lives within the very flame of love
   A kind of wick or snuff that will abate it ;
   And nothing is at a like goodness still,
   For goodness, growing to a plurisy,
   Dies in his own too much : that we would do
   We should do when we would ; for this ' would '
       changes
   And hath abatements and delays as many   120
   As there are tongues, are hands, are accidents,
   And then this ' should ' is like a spendthrift's sigh,
   That hurts by easing.   But, to the quick o' the ulcer :]
   Hamlet comes back : what would you undertake,
   To show yourself indeed your father's son
   More than in words ?

Lae.   To cut his throat i' the church.

Ki. No place indeed should murder sanctuarize ;

Revenge should have no bounds.   But, good Laertes,
Will you do this, keep close within your chamber.
Hamlet return'd shall know you are come home :   130
We 'll put on those shall praise your excellence
And set a double varnish on the fame
The Frenchman gave you ; bring you in fine together
And wager o'er your heads : he, being remiss,
Most generous, and free from all contriving,
Will not peruse the foils, so that with ease,
Or with a little shuffling, you may choose
A sword unbated, and in a pass of practice
Requite him for your father.

Lae.   I will do 't ;
And for that purpose I 'll anoint my sword.   140
I bought an unction of a mountebank,
So mortal, that but dip a knife in it,
Where it draws blood, no cataplasm so rare,
Collected from all simples that have virtue
Under the moon, can save the thing from death
That is but scratch'd withal : I 'll touch my point
With this contagion, that, if I gall him slightly,
It may be death.

Ki.   Let 's further think of this ;
Weigh what convenience both of time and means
May fit us to our shape : if this should fail,   150

141

And that our drift look through our bad performance,
'Twere better not assay'd : therefore this project
Should have a back or second, that might hold
If this did blast in proof.   Soft ! let me see :
We 'll make a solemn wager on your cunnings :
I ha 't :
When in your motion you are hot and dry—
As make your bouts more violent to that end—
And that he calls for drink, I 'll have prepar'd him
A chalice for the nonce, whereon but sipping,   160
If he by chance escape your venom'd stuck,
Our purpose may hold there.   [But stay, what noise ?]

Enter Queen

[How now, sweet queen ?]

Qu.   One woe doth tread upon another's heel,
So fast they follow : your sister 's drown'd, Laertes.

Lae.   Drown'd !   O, where ?

Qu.   There is a willow grows ascaunt the brook,
That shows his hoar leaves in the glassy stream ;
Therewith fantastic garlands did she make
Of crow-flowers, nettles, daisies, and long purples,   170
That liberal shepherds give a grosser name,
But our cold maids do dead men's fingers call them :
There, on the pendent boughs her crownet weeds
Clambering to hang, an envious sliver broke,

When down her weedy trophies and herself
Fell in the weeping brook, her clothes spread wide,
And mermaid-like a while they bore her up :
Which time she chanted snatches of old lauds,
As one incapable of her own distress,
Or like a creature native and indued   180
Unto that element : but long it could not be
Till that her garments, heavy with their drink,
Pull'd the poor wretch from her melodious lay
To muddy death.

Lae.   Alas, then she is drown'd !

Qu. Drown'd, drown'd.

Lae. Too much of water hast thou, poor Ophelia,
And therefore I forbid my tears : but yet
It is our trick : nature her custom holds,
Let shame say what it will : when these are gone,
The woman will be out.   Adieu, my lord :   190
I have a speech afire that fain would blaze,
But that this folly douts it.   *Exit*

Ki.   Let 's follow, Gertrude :
How much I had to do to calm his rage !
Now fear I this will give it start again ;
Therefore let 's follow.   *Exeunt*

Act Fifth

SCENE I

The next day

A churchyard

Enter two Clowns, with spades, &c.

First Clo. Is she to be buried in Christian burial when she wilfully seeks her own salvation?

Sec. Clo. I tell thee she is; therefore make her grave straight: the crowner hath sat on her, and finds it Christian burial.

First Clo. How can that be, unless she drown'd herself in her own defence?

Sec. Clo. Why, 'tis found so.

First Clo. It must be 'so offended;' it cannot be else. †
For here lies the point: if I drown myself wittingly, 10
it argues an act: and an act hath three branches; it
is, to act, to do, to perform, argal she drown'd
herself wittingly.

Sec. Clo. Nay, but hear you, goodman delver.

First Clo. Give me leave. Here lies the water; good:
here stands the man; good: if the man go to this

water and drown himself, it is, will he, nill he, he
goes, mark you that ; but if the water come to him
and drown him, he drowns not himself : argal, he
that is not guilty of his own death shortens not his   20
own life.

Sec. Clo. But is this law ?

First Clo. Ay, marry, is 't ; crowner's quest law.

Sec. Clo. Will you ha' the truth on 't ? If this had not
been a gentlewoman, she should have been buried
out o' Christian burial.

First Clo. Why, there thou say'st : and the more pity
that great folk should have countenance in this
world to drown or hang themselves, more than
their even Christian. Come, my spade ; there is   30
no ancient gentlemen but gardeners, ditchers, and
grave-makers : they hold up Adam's profession.

Sec. Clo. Was he a gentleman ?

First Clo 'A was the first that ever bore arms.

{*Sec. Clo.* Why, he had none.

First Clo. What, art a heathen ? How dost thou understand the Scripture ? The Scripture says Adam
digg'd : could he dig without arms ?} I 'll put
another question to thee : if thou answerest me not
to the purpose, confess thyself—   40

Sec. Clo. Go to.

First Clo. What is he that builds stronger than either the mason, the shipwright, or the carpenter?

Sec. Clo. The gallows-maker; for that outlives a thousand tenants.

First Clo. I like thy wit well, in good faith: the gallows does well; but how does it well? it does well to those that do ill: now, thou dost ill to say the gallows is built stronger than the church: argal, the gallows may do well to thee. To't again, come.　　50

Sec. Clo. 'Who builds stronger than a mason, a shipwright, or a carpenter?'

First Clo. Ay, tell me that, and unyoke.

Sec. Clo. Marry, now I can tell.

First Clo. To't.

Sec. Clo. Mass, I cannot tell.

First Clo. Cudgel thy brains no more about it, for your dull ass will not mend his pace with beating, and when you are ask'd this question next, say 'a grave-maker: the houses he makes lasts till doomsday.'　60
Go, get thee in, and fetch me a stoup of liquor.　　†

Exit Sec. Clo.
He digs, and sings

In youth, when I did love, did love,
　　Methought it was very sweet

146

To contract, O, the time, for-a my behove,
O, methought, there-a was nothing-a meet.
Enter Hamlet and Horatio

Ham. Has this fellow no feeling of his business ?   'A
sings in grave-making.

Hor. Custom hath made it in him a property of easiness.

Ham. 'Tis e'en so : the hand of little employment hath
the daintier sense.   70

First Clo. (*sings*) But age, with his stealing steps
Hath clawed me in his clutch,
And hath shipped me into the land,
As if I had never been such.

Throws up a skull

Ham. That skull had a tongue in it, and could sing once :
how the knave jowls it to the ground, as if 'twere
Cain's jaw-bone, that did the first murder ! This
might be the pate of a politician, which this ass
now o'er-reaches ; one that would circumvent God,
might it not ?   80

Hor. It might, my lord.

Ham. Or of a courtier, which could say 'Good morrow,
sweet lord ? How dost thou, sweet lord ?' This
might be my lord such-a-one, that prais'd my lord
such-a-one's horse, when 'a went to beg it, might it
not ?

147

Hor. Ay, my lord.

Ham. Why, e'en so : and now my Lady Worm's, chop-
less, and knocked about the mazzard with a sexton's
spade : here 's fine revolution, an we had the trick to   90
see 't ; did these bones cost no more the breeding,
but to play at loggits with them ? mine ache to
think on 't.

First Clo. (*sings*) A pick-axe, and a spade, a spade,
    For and a shrouding sheet :
    O, a pit of clay for to be made
    For such a guest is meet.

        Throws up another skull

Ham. There 's another : why may not that be the skull of
a lawyer ? Where be his quiddities now, his quillets,
his cases, his tenures, and his tricks ? why does he   100
suffer this mad knave now to knock him about the
sconce with a dirty shovel, and will not tell him of
his action of battery ? Hum ! This fellow might †
be in 's time a great buyer of land, with his statutes,
his recognizances, his fines, his double vouchers, his
recoveries : {is this the fine of his fines and the re-
covery of his recoveries,} to have his fine pate full
of fine dirt ? will vouchers vouch him no more of
his purchases, and doubles, than the length and
breadth of a pair of indentures ? The very convey-   110

ances of his lands will scarcely lie in this box, and
must the inheritor himself have no more, ha ?

Hor. Not a jot more, my lord.

Ham. Is not parchment made of sheep-skins ?

Hor. Ay, my lord, and of calves-skins too.

Ham. They are sheep and calves which seek out assurance
in that. I will speak to this fellow. Whose grave 's
this, sirrah ?

First Clo. Mine, sir.

> (*sings*) Or a pit of clay for to be made   120
> {For such a guest is meet.}

Ham. I think it be thine indeed, for thou liest in 't.

First Clo. You lie out on 't, sir, and therefore 'tis not
yours : for my part, I do not lie in 't, and yet it is
mine.

Ham. Thou dost lie in 't, to be in 't and say it is thine :
'tis for the dead, not for the quick ; therefore thou
liest.

First Clo. 'Tis a quick lie, sir ; 'twill away again from me
to you.   130

Ham. What man dost thou dig it for ?

First Clo. For no man, sir.

Ham. What woman then ?

First Clo. For none neither.

M

Ham. Who is to be buried in 't?

First Clo. One that was a woman, sir; but, rest her soul, she 's dead.

Ham. How absolute the knave is! we must speak by the card, or equivocation will undo us. ~~By the Lord,~~ Horatio, this three years I have took note of it, the 140 age is grown so pick'd, that the toe of the peasant comes so near the heel of the courtier, he galls his kibe. How long hast thou been grave-maker?

First Clo. Of the days i' the year I came to 't that day that our last king Hamlet overcame Fortinbras.

Ham. How long is that since?

First Clo. Cannot you tell that? every fool can tell that: it was that very day that young Hamlet was born: he that is mad, and sent into England.

Ham. Ay, marry, why was he sent into England? 150

First Clo. Why, because 'a was mad; 'a shall recover his wits there; or, if 'a do not, 'tis no great matter there.

Ham. Why?

First Clo. 'Twill not be seen in him there; there the men are as mad as he.

Ham. How came he mad?

First Clo. Very strangely, they say.

Ham. How 'strangely'?

First Clo. Faith, e'en with losing his wits.

Ham. Upon what ground?

First Clo. Why, here in Denmark: I have been sexton here, man and boy, thirty years.

Ham. How long will a man lie i' the earth ere he rot?

First Clo. I' faith if 'a be not rotten before 'a die—as we have many pocky corses {now-a-days,} that will scarce hold the laying in—'a will last you some eight year or nine year: a tanner will last you nine year.

Ham. Why he more than another?

First Clo. Why, sir, his hide is so tann'd with his trade 170 that 'a will keep out water a great while; and your water is a sore decayer of your whoreson dead body. Here's a skull now hath lien you i' the earth three and twenty years.

Ham. Whose was it?

First Clo. A whoreson mad fellow's it was; whose do you think it was?

Ham. Nay, I know not.

First Clo. A pestilence on him for a mad rogue! 'a pour'd a flagon of Rhenish on my head once. This 180 same skull, sir, was, sir, Yorick's skull, the king's jester.

Ham. This?

First Clo. E'en that.

Ham. {Let me see.} (*Takes the skull.*) Alas, poor Yorick!
I knew him, Horatio, a fellow of infinite jest, of most
excellent fancy: he hath borne me on his back a
thousand times, and now how abhorred in my
imagination it is! my gorge rises at it. Here hung
those lips that I have kiss'd I know not how oft; 190
where be your gibes now? your gambols, your
songs, your flashes of merriment, that were wont to
set the table on a roar? Not one now to mock your
own grinning, quite chop-fallen. Now get you to
my lady's table, and tell her, let her paint an inch
thick, to this favour she must come; make her laugh
at that. Prithee, Horatio, tell me one thing.

Hor. What's that, my lord?

Ham. Dost thou think Alexander looked o' this fashion
i' the earth? 200

Hor. E'en so.

Ham. And smelt so? pah!   *Puts down the skull*

Hor. E'en so, my lord.

Ham. To what base uses we may return, Horatio! Why
may not imagination trace the noble dust of Alexander, till 'a find it stopping a bung-hole?

Hor. 'Twere to consider too curiously, to consider so.

Ham. No, faith, not a jot; but to follow him thither
with modesty enough, and likelihood to lead it: {as

thus :} Alexander died, Alexander was buried, Alex-   210
ander returneth to dust, the dust is earth, of earth we
make loam, and why of that loam, whereto he was
converted, might they not stop a beer-barrel ?

Imperious Cæsar, dead and turn'd to clay,
Might stop a hole, to keep the wind away.
O, that that earth, which kept the world in awe,
Should patch a wall to expel the winter's flaw !

But soft ! but soft, awhile : here comes the king.
    Enter the Corpse of Ophelia, a Priest, King, Queen,
        Laertes, Courtiers
The queen, the courtiers : who is this they follow ?
And with such maimed rites ?   This doth betoken   220
The corse they follow did with desperate hand
Fordo its own life : 'twas of some estate.
Couch we awhile, and mark.   *Retiring with Horatio*

Lae. What ceremony else ?

Ham. That is Laertes, a very noble youth : mark.

Lae. What ceremony else ?

Pr. Her obsequies have been as far enlarg'd
    As we have warranty : her death was doubtful,
    And, but that great command o'ersways the order,
    She should in ground unsanctified been lodg'd   230
    Till the last trumpet ; for charitable prayers,

{Shards,} flints and pebbles should be thrown on her:
Yet here she is allow'd her virgin crants,
Her maiden strewments, and the bringing home
Of bell and burial.

Lae. Must there no more be done?

Pr.   No more be done:
We should profane the service of the dead
To sing a requiem and such rest to her
As to peace-parted souls.

Lae.   Lay her i' the earth,
And from her fair and unpolluted flesh   240
May violets spring! I tell thee, churlish priest,
A minist'ring angel shall my sister be,
When thou liest howling.

Ham.   What, the fair Ophelia!

Qu. (*scattering flowers*) Sweets to the sweet: farewell!
I hop'd thou shouldst have been my Hamlet's wife,
I thought thy bride-bed to have deck'd, sweet maid,
And not have strew'd thy grave.

Lae.   O, treble woe
Fall ten times double on that cursed head
Whose wicked deed thy most ingenious sense
Depriv'd thee of! Hold off the earth a while,   250
Till I have caught her once more in mine arms:

                    Leaps into the grave

Now pile your dust upon the quick and dead,
Till of this flat a mountain you have made
To o'ertop old Pelion, or the skyish head
Of blue Olympus.

Ham. (*advancing*)   What is he whose grief
Bears such an emphasis ? whose phrase of sorrow
Conjures the wand'ring stars, and makes them stand
Like wonder-wounded hearers ?   This is I,
Hamlet the Dane.   *Leaps into the grave*

Lae. The devil take thy soul !   *Grappling with him*

Ham.   Thou pray'st not well.   260
I prithee take thy fingers from my throat ;
For, though I am not splenitive and rash,
Yet have I in me something dangerous,
Which let thy wisdom fear.   Hold off thy hand.

Ki. Pluck them asunder.

Qu.   Hamlet, Hamlet !

All.   Gentlemen,—

Hor. Good my lord, be quiet.

                    *The Attendants part them, and they
                        come out of the grave*

Ham. Why, I will fight with him upon this theme
Until my eyelids will no longer wag.

Qu. O my son, what theme ?

Ham. I lov'd Ophelia : forty thousand brothers   270

Could not, with all their quantity of love,
Make up my sum.   What wilt thou do for her?

Ki. O, he is mad, Laertes.

Qu. For love of God, forbear him.

Ham. 'Swounds, show me what thou 'lt do:

Woo 't weep? woo 't fight? [woo 't fast?] woo 't
   tear thyself?

Woo 't drink up esill? eat a crocodile?

I 'll do 't.   Dost come here to whine?

To outface me with leaping in her grave?

Be buried quick with her, and so will I: 280

And, if thou prate of mountains, let them throw

Millions of acres on us, till our ground,

Singeing his pate against the burning zone,

Make Ossa like a wart!   Nay, an thou 'lt mouth,

I 'll rant as well as thou.

Qu.   This is mere madness:

And thus a while the fit will work on him;

Anon, as patient as the female dove

When that her golden couplets are disclos'd,

His silence will sit drooping.

Ham.   Hear you, sir;

What is the reason that you use me thus?   290

I lov'd you ever: but it is no matter;

Let Hercules himself do what he may,

The cat will mew, and dog will have his day. *Exit*

Ki. I pray thee, good Horatio, wait upon him.

Exit Horatio

(*to Laertes*) Strengthen your patience in our last
   night's speech ;

We 'll put the matter to the present push.

Good Gertrude, set some watch over your son.

This grave shall have a living monument :

An hour of quiet shortly shall we see ;

Till then in patience our proceeding be.   *Exeunt* 300

SCENE II

A hall in the castle

Enter Hamlet and Horatio

Ham. So much for this, sir : now shall you see the other ;
   You do remember all the circumstance ?

Hor. Remember it, my lord !

Ham. Sir, in my heart there was a kind of fighting,
   That would not let me sleep : methought I lay
   Worse than the mutines in the bilbo.   Rashly,
   And prais'd be rashness for it, let us know,
   Our indiscretion sometime serves us well
   When our deep plots do pall, and that should learn us

157

There's a divinity that shapes our ends,   10
Rough-hew them how we will,

Hor.   That is most certain.

Ham. Up from my cabin,
My sea-gown scarf'd about me, in the dark
Grop'd I to find out them, had my desire,
Finger'd their packet, and in fine withdrew
To mine own room again ; making so bold,
My fears forgetting manners, to unseal
Their grand commission ; where I found, Horatio,
A royal knavery, an exact command,
Larded with many several sorts of reasons,   20
Importing Denmark's health, and England's too,
With, ho ! such bugs and goblins in my life,
That, on the supervise, no leisure bated,
No, not to stay the grinding of the axe,
My head should be struck off.

Hor.   Is't possible ?

Ham. Here's the commission, read it at more leisure.
But wilt thou hear now how I did proceed ?

Hor. I beseech you.

Ham. Being thus be-netted round with villanies,—
Or I could make a prologue to my brains,   30
They had begun the play,—I sat me down,
Devis'd a new commission, wrote it fair:

I once did hold it, as our statists do,
A baseness to write fair, and labour'd much
How to forget that learning, but, sir, now
It did me yeoman's service : wilt thou know
The effect of what I wrote ?

Hor.   Ay, good my lord.

Ham. An earnest conjuration from the king,
As England was his faithful tributary,
As love between them like the palm might flourish,   40
As peace should still her wheaten garland wear
And stand a comma 'tween their amities,
And many such-like 'As'es' of great charge,
That, on the view and knowing of these contents,
Without debatement further, more or less,
He should those bearers put to sudden death,
Not shriving-time allow'd.

Hor.   How was this seal'd ?

Ham. Why, even in that was heaven ordinant.
I had my father's signet in my purse,
Which was the model of that Danish seal :   50
Folded the writ up in the form of the other,
Subscrib'd it, gave 't the impression, plac'd it
    safely,
The changeling never known.   Now, the next day
Was our sea-fight ; and what to this was sequent

Thou know'st already.

Hor. So Guildenstern and Rosencrantz go to 't.

Ham. {Why, man, they did make love to this employ-
       ment ;}

They are not near my conscience ; their defeat
Does by their own insinuation grow :
'Tis dangerous when the baser nature comes   60
Between the pass and fell incensed points
Of mighty opposites.

Hor.   Why, what a king is this !

Ham. Does it not, think'st thee, stand me now upon—
He that hath kill'd my king, and whor'd my mother,
Popp'd in between the election and my hopes,
Thrown out his angle for my proper life,
And with such cozenage—is 't not perfect conscience,
{To quit him with this arm ? and is 't not to be
       damn'd,
To let this canker of our nature come
In further evil ?   70

Hor. It must be shortly known to him from England
What is the issue of the business there.

Ham. It will be short : the interim is mine ;
And a man's life 's no more than to say ' One.'
But I am very sorry, good Horatio,
That to Laertes I forgot myself ;

For, by the image of my cause, I see
The portraiture of his : I'll court his favours :
But, sure, the bravery of his grief did put me
Into a towering passion.

Hor.   Peace ! who comes here ?}   80
                Enter Osric

Osr. Your lordship is right welcome back to Denmark.

Ham. I humbly thank you, sir. (*to Hor.*) Dost know
this water-fly ?

Hor. No, my good lord.

Ham. Thy state is the more gracious, for 'tis a vice to
know him.   He hath much land, and fertile : let a
beast be lord of beasts, and his crib shall stand at the
king's mess : 'tis a chough, but, as I say, spacious in
the possession of dirt.

Osr. Sweet lord, if your lordship were at leisure, I should   90
impart a thing to you from his majesty.

Ham. I will receive it, sir, with all diligence of spirit.
Your bonnet to his right use, 'tis for the head.

Osr. I thank your lordship, it is very hot.

Ham. No, believe me, 'tis very cold, the wind is northerly.

Osr. It is indifferent cold, my lord, indeed.

Ham. But yet methinks it is very sultry and hot, or my
complexion—

Osr. Exceedingly, my lord ; it is very sultry, as 'twere

I cannot tell how : my lord, his majesty bade me 100
signify to you that he has laid a great wager on your
head : sir, this is the matter—

Ham. I beseech you, remember—

Hamlet moves him to put on his hat

Osr. Nay, good my lord, for my ease, in good faith.
[Sir, here is newly come to court Laertes ; believe
me, an absolute gentleman, full of most excellent
differences, of very soft society, and great showing :
indeed, to speak sellingly of him, he is the card or
calendar of gentry ; for you shall find in him the
continent of what parts a gentleman would see. 110

Ham. Sir, his definement suffers no perdition in you,
though, I know, to divide him inventorially would
dizzy the arithmetic of memory, and yet but yaw
neither, in respect of his quick sail. But in the verity
of extolment, I take him to be a soul of great article,
and his infusion of such dearth and rareness, as, to
make true diction of him, his semblable is his mirror,
and who else would trace him, his umbrage, nothing
more.

Osr. Your lordship speaks most infallibly of him. 120

Ham. The concernancy, sir ? why do we wrap the gentleman in our more rawer breath ?

Osr. Sir ?

Sir you are not ignorant of what
excellence is at his weapon

Hor. Is 't not possible to understand in another tongue ?
You will to 't, sir, really.

Ham. What imports the nomination of this gentleman ?

Osr. Of Laertes ?

Hor. His purse is empty already ; all 's golden words are
spent.

Ham. Of him, sir. 130

Osr. I know you are not ignorant—

Ham. I would you did, sir : yet, in faith, if you did, it
would not much approve me.   Well, sir ?]

Osr. You are not ignorant of what excellence Laertes
is—

[*Ham.* I dare not confess that, lest I should compare with †
him in excellence ; but to know a man well were to
know himself.

Osr. I mean, sir, for his weapon ; but in the imputation
laid on him, by them in his meed, he 's unfellow'd.] 140

Ham. What 's his weapon ?

Osr. Rapier and dagger.

Ham. That 's two of his weapons : but, well.

Osr. The king, sir, hath wager'd with him six Barbary
horses, against the which he has impawn'd, as I take
it, six French rapiers and poniards, with their assigns,
as girdle, hanger, and so : three of the carriages, in
faith, are very dear to fancy, very responsive to the

hilts, most delicate carriages, and of very liberal
conceit.   150

Ham. What call you the carriages?

[*Hor.* I knew you must be edified by the margent ere you
had done.]

Osr. The carriages, sir, are the hangers.

Ham. The phrase would be more germane to the matter
if we could carry a cannon by our sides: I would it
be hangers till then. But on: six Barbary horses
against six French swords, their assigns, and three
liberal-conceited carriages; that's the French bet
against the Danish. Why is this all you call it?   160

Osr. The king, sir, hath laid, sir, that in a dozen passes
between yourself and him, he shall not exceed you
three hits: he hath laid on twelve for nine; and
it would come to immediate trial if your lordship
would vouchsafe the answer.

Ham. How if I answer 'no'?

Osr. I mean, my lord, the opposition of your person in trial.

Ham. Sir, I will walk here in the hall: if it please his
majesty (it is the breathing time of day with me) let
the foils be brought, the gentleman willing, and the   170
king hold his purpose, I will win for him an I can: if
not, I will gain nothing but my shame, and the odd hits.

Osr. Shall I deliver you so?

Ham. To this effect, sir, after what flourish your nature will.

Osr. I commend my duty to your lordship.

Ham. Yours, {yours.} (*exit Osric.*) He does well to commend it himself; there are no tongues else for 's turn.

Hor. This lapwing runs away with the shell on his head.

Ham. 'A did comply with his dug before he sucked it. †
Thus has he—and many more of the same breed that 180
I know the drossy age dotes on—only got the tune
of the time and outward habit of encounter ; a kind
of yesty collection, which carries them through and
through the most fond and winnowed opinions ; and
do but blow them to their trial, the bubbles are out.

[*Enter a Lord*

Lo. My lord, his majesty commended him to you by
young Osric, who brings back to him, that you attend him in the hall : he sends to know if your
pleasure hold to play with Laertes, or that you will
take longer time ? 190

Ham. I am constant to my purposes ; they follow the
king's pleasure : if his fitness speaks, mine is ready ;
now or whensoever, provided I be so able as now.

Lo. The king and queen and all are coming down.

Ham. In happy time.

Lo. The queen desires you to use some gentle entertainment to Laertes before you fall to play.

N 165

Ham. ~~She well instructs me.~~   *Exit Lord*]

Hor. You will lose, my lord.

Ham. I do not think so ; since he went into France, I have 200
been in continual practice ; I shall win at the odds.
Thou wouldst not think how ill all 's here about my
heart, but it is no matter.

Hor. Nay, good my lord,—

Ham. It is but foolery ; but it is such a kind of gain-giving †
as would perhaps trouble a woman.

Hor. If your mind dislike any thing, obey it.   I will fore-
stal their repair hither, and say you are not fit.

Ham. Not a whit ; we defy augury : there is special
providence in the fall of a sparrow.   If it be now,
'tis not to come ; if it be not to come, it will be now ; 210
if it be not now, yet it will come : the readiness is
all ; since no man of ought he leaves, knows what †
is 't to leave betimes, let be.

[*A table prepared ; trumpets, drums, and Officers with cushions :
King, Queen, and all the State ; foils, daggers, and
Laertes*]

{*Enter King, Queen, Laertes, and Lords, Osric and other
Attendants with foils and gauntlets ; a table and flagons
of wine on it*}   †

Ki. Come, Hamlet, come, and take this hand from me.

                    The King puts Laertes' hand into Hamlet's

Ham. Give me your pardon, sir : I have done you wrong ;
But pardon 't, as you are a gentleman.
This presence knows,
And you must needs have heard, how I am punish'd
With a sore distraction.   What I have done,   220
That might your nature, honour, and exception
Roughly awake, I here proclaim was madness.
Was 't Hamlet wrong'd Laertes ?   Never Hamlet.
If Hamlet from himself be ta'en away,
And when he 's not himself does wrong Laertes,
Then Hamlet does it not, Hamlet denies it.
Who does it then ?   His madness.   If 't be so,
Hamlet is of the faction that is wrong'd ;
His madness is poor Hamlet's enemy.
{Sir, in this audience,}   230
Let my disclaiming from a purpos'd evil
Free me so far in your most generous thoughts,
That I have shot my arrow o'er the house,
And hurt my brother.

Lae.   I am satisfied in nature,   †
Whose motive, in this case, should stir me most
To my revenge : but in my terms of honour
I stand aloof, and will no reconcilement,
Till by some elder masters of known honour
I have a voice and precedent of peace,

To keep my name ungor'd.   But all that time   240
I do receive your offer'd love like love
And will not wrong it.

Ham.   I embrace it freely,
And will this brother's wager frankly play.
Give us the foils. {Come on.}

Lae.   Come, one for me.

Ham. I 'll be your foil, Laertes : in mine ignorance
Your skill shall, like a star i' the darkest night,
Stick fiery off indeed.

Lae.   You mock me, sir.

Ham. No, by this hand.

Ki. Give them the foils, young Osric.   Cousin Hamlet,
You know the wager ?

Ham.   Very well, my lord ;   250
Your grace has laid the odds o' the weaker side.

Ki. I do not fear it ; I have seen you both :
But since he is better, we have therefore odds.

Lae. This is too heavy ; let me see another.

Ham. This likes me well.   These foils have all a length ?

They prepare to play

Osr. Ay, my good lord.

Ki. Set me the stoups of wine upon that table.
If Hamlet give the first or second hit,
Or quit in answer of the third exchange,

168

Let all the battlements their ordnance fire ;   260
The king shall drink to Hamlet's better breath,
And in the cup an union shall he throw,
Richer than that which four successive kings
In Denmark's crown have worn.   Give me the cups ;
And let the kettle to the trumpet speak,
The trumpet to the cannoneer without,
The cannons to the heavens, the heaven to earth,
' Now the king drinks to Hamlet.'   Come, begin ;
And you, the judges, bear a wary eye.

Trumpets the while

Ham. Come on, sir.

Lae.   Come, my lord.   *They play*

Ham.   One.

Lae.   No.

Ham.   Judgement.   270

Osr. A hit, a very palpable hit.

Drum, trumpets, and shot
Flourish, a piece goes off

Lae.   Well, again.

Ki. Stay, give me drink.   Hamlet, this pearl is thine ;
Here's to thy health ;   give him the cup.

Ham. I'll play this bout first, set it by a while.
Come. (*They play.*) Another hit ; what say you ?

Lae. {A touch, a touch,} I do confess 't.

169

Ki. Our son shall win.

Qu. He 's fat and scant of breath.   †
Here, Hamlet, take my napkin, rub thy brows :
The queen carouses to thy fortune, Hamlet.

Ham. Good madam !

Ki. Gertrude, do not drink.   280

Qu. I will, my lord ; I pray you, pardon me.

Ki. (*aside*) It is the poison'd cup ; it is too late.

Ham. I dare not drink yet, madam ; by and by.

Qu. Come, let me wipe thy face.

Lae. My lord, I 'll hit him now.

Ki. I do not think 't.

Lae. (*aside*) And yet it is almost against my conscience.

Ham. Come for the third, Laertes : you do but dally ;
I pray you, pass with your best violence ;
I am afeard you make a wanton of me.

Lae. Say you so ? come on.   *They play* 290

Osr. Nothing neither way.

Lae. Have at you now !

      Laertes wounds Hamlet ; then, in scuffling, they †
        change rapiers, and Hamlet wounds Laertes

Ki. Part them ; they are incens'd.

Ham. Nay, come, again.   *The Queen falls*

Osr. Look to the queen there, ho !

Hor. They bleed on both sides. How is it, my lord ?

Osr. How is 't, Laertes ?

Lae. Why, as a woodcock to mine own springe, Osric ;
I am justly kill'd with mine own treachery.

Ham. How does the queen ?

Ki.   She swounds to see them bleed.

Qu. No, no, the drink, the drink,—O my dear Hamlet,—
The drink, the drink !   I am poison'd.   *Dies* 300

Ham. O villany !   Ho ! let the door be lock'd :
Treachery !   seek it out.   *Laertes falls*

Lae. It is here, Hamlet : {Hamlet,} thou art slain ;
No medicine in the world can do thee good,
In thee there is not half an hour's life ;
The treacherous instrument is in thy hand,
Unbated and envenom'd : the foul practice
Hath turn'd itself on me ; lo, here I lie,
Never to rise again : thy mother 's poison'd :
I can no more : the king, the king 's to blame.   310

Ham. The point envenom'd too !
Then, venom, to thy work.   *Stabs the King*

All. Treason !   treason !

Ki. O, yet defend me, friends ; I am but hurt.

Ham. Here, thou incestuous, {murderous,} damned Dane,
Drink off this potion : is thy union here ?
Follow my mother.   *King dies*

Lae.   He is justly serv'd ;

It is a poison temper'd by himself.
Exchange forgiveness with me, noble Hamlet:
Mine and my father's death come not upon thee,   320
Nor thine on me!   *Dies*

Ham. Heaven make thee free of it! I follow thee.
I am dead, Horatio. Wretched queen, adieu!
You that look pale, and tremble at this chance,
That are but mutes or audience to this act,
Had I but time—as this fell sergeant death
Is strict in his arrest—O, I could tell you—
But let it be. Horatio, I am dead;
Thou livest; report me and my cause aright
To the unsatisfied.

Hor.   Never believe it: 330
I am more an antique Roman than a Dane,
Here's yet some liquor left.

Ham.   As thou 'rt a man,
Give me the cup: let go, by heaven I 'll have 't.
O God, Horatio, what a wounded name,
Things standing thus unknown, shall I leave behind me!
If thou didst ever hold me in thy heart,
Absent thee from felicity a while,
And in this harsh world draw thy breath in pain,
To tell my story.   *March afar off*
      What warlike noise is this?

Osr. Young Fortinbras, with conquest come from Poland,   340
　　　To the ambassadors of England gives
　　　This warlike volley.

Ham.　　　　　　　O, I die, Horatio;
　　　The potent poison quite o'er-crows my spirit:
　　　I cannot live to hear the news from England,
　　　But I do prophesy the election lights
　　　On Fortinbras: he has my dying voice;
　　　So tell him, with the occurrents, more and less,
　　　Which have solicited.   The rest is silence.
　　　　{O, o, o, o!}　　　　　　　　*Dies*

Hor. Now cracks a noble heart.   Good night, sweet
　　　　prince,
　　　And flights of angels sing thee to thy rest !　　　350
　　　　　　　　　　　　　　March within
　　　Why does the drum come hither?
　　　　*Enter Fortinbras, and the English Ambassadors, with
　　　　　　drum, colours, and Attendants*

For. Where is this sight?

Hor.　　　　　　　What is it you would see?
　　　If aught of woe, or wonder, cease your search.

For. This quarry cries on havoc.   O proud death,
　　　What feast is toward in thine eternal cell,
　　　That thou so many princes at a shot
　　　So bloodily hast struck?

173

First Amb.   The sight is dismal ;
And our affairs from England come too late :
The ears are senseless that should give us hearing,
To tell him his commandment is fulfill'd,   360
That Rosencrantz and Guildenstern are dead :
Where should we have our thanks ?

Hor.   Not from his mouth
Had it the ability of life to thank you :
He never gave commandment for their death.
But since, so jump upon this bloody question,
You from the Polack wars, and you from England,
Are here arriv'd, give order that these bodies
High on a stage be placed to the view,
And let me speak to the yet unknowing world
How these things came about : so shall you hear   370
Of carnal, bloody and unnatural acts,
Of accidental judgements, casual slaughters,
Of deaths put on by cunning and forc'd cause,   †
And, in this upshot, purposes mistook
Fall'n on the inventors' heads : all this can I
Truly deliver.

For.   Let us haste to hear it,
And call the noblest to the audience.
For me, with sorrow I embrace my fortune :
I have some rights of memory in this kingdom,

Which now to claim my vantage doth invite me.   380

Hor. Of that I shall have also cause to speak,
And from his mouth whose voice will draw on more :
But let this same be presently perform'd,
Even while men's minds are wild, lest more mischance
On plots and errors happen.

For.   Let four captains
Bear Hamlet like a soldier to the stage,
For he was likely, had he been put on,
To have proved most royal : and, for his passage,
The soldiers' music and the rite of war
Speak loudly for him.   390
Take up the bodies : such a sight as this
Becomes the field, but here shows much amiss.
Go, bid the soldiers shoot.

                                        Exeunt

Notes

I. i. 63. *sleaded pollax*; so Q 2 (and Q 1). F reads *sledded Pollax*. The usual reading, *sledded Polacks*, and its interpretation, that he fell upon the sledged Poles, seem to me equally untenable. In the first place it is odd that Q 2, having just printed *Norway* normally in italics, should two lines lower print a proper name in roman and with a lowercase initial; and not less odd when we find in II. ii. 75 the normal singular normally printed *Pollacke*, and in V. ii. 369 *Pollack*. In the second place, as a matter of behaviour, it is odd that he should fall upon his enemies in a 'parle' however angry, and, even if he did, even odder that in the heat and rapid movement of action what should be noticed about him was his frown. It seems to me clear that the picture is of a man frowning in anger and striking his poleaxe on the ice. *Sleaded* is still difficult. Just possibly we should read *his loaded* for *the sleaded*.

I. ii. 65. *A little more than kin . . .*; it is oddly appropriate that Hamlet's first words should be a word-play on which the commentators are equally divergent and indecisive. Perhaps ' a little more than a mere kinsman (cousin), but a son only by the unnatural and incestuous relation of the king to his mother' is as satisfactory as any. The *i' the sun* is clear enough, first in its obvious meaning, and secondly ' in the relation of a son '; but it is obscured by modern spelling, *sonne* in Elizabethan spelling being used indifferently for *son* and *sun*.

I. ii. 129. *sullied*; Q 2 (and Q 1) *sallied*. F *solid*. Cf. II. i. 39, where Q 2 reads *sallies* for the clearly correct *sullies*, and also *L. L. L.*

V. ii. 353. where Q reads *unsallied lilly*. There seems no reason at all for abandoning Q 2, particularly as in Hamlet's state of mind the sulliedness of flesh is troubling him much more than its solidity.

I. ii. 163. Emphasis surely on both *friend* and *that* (*i.e.* the relation is friend and friend, not prince and servant).

I. ii. 228. *Then saw you not his face.* so Q 2. Most editions take F's reading *face?*, surely wrongly, since the implication of the cap-a-pie arming is that his face would be hidden, and the question has the wrong turn.

I. iii. 18. A Folio addition which reads almost like an explanatory gloss.

I. iii. 21. *safety*; so Q 2. F reads *sanctity*, and Theobald conjectured *sanity*. *Safety*, though used as a trisyllable by Spenser is disyllabic in Shakespeare (see, *e.g.*, l. 43 below). The easiest regularisation is the insertion of *the* before *health*.

I. iii. 65. *comrade*; so F. Q 2 (also Q 1) *courage*. It is impossible to be happy about the F emendation, since though the *u : m* confusion is easy enough, the *d : g.* is not; and for *courage* see O.E.D.

I. iii. 73. A vexed passage: the most tempting emendation is the omission of *of a*; but it is obstinately there, in all three texts: the least unsatisfactory is probably Dover Wilson's, *Are often most . . .* And I fancy that *chief* may be a correction of *best* which has found its way into the wrong line.

I. iii. 83. *The time invites you; go*; so F. Q 2 reads *The time invests you goe*, as though *invests* carried the meaning of 'urges you to.'

I. iv. 36-38. A famous crux. F gives us no help since it omits the passage. Dover Wilson treats it by the same method as the last difficulty, reading *often* for *of a*. *Eale* is thus a misreading of *eule* (i.e. *evil*; cf. *deule* for *devil* in III. ii. 129, and the misprint *deale* in II. ii. 601) and *doubt* a variant spelling of *dout* (*i.e.* put out, cf. *this folly doubts it*, IV. vii. 192, F reading). And we have

> the dram of evil
> Doth all the noble substance often dout
> To his own scandle.

Which is ingenious and graphically possible. But it is not so satisfactory in sense. A flame can be 'douted': but how can a 'noble substance' be 'douted,' and, if so, why by a dram? The sense required is infection rather than extinction. However, the general sense of the passage is clear enough.

I. iv. 71. *bettles*; so Q 2 (Q 1 *beckles*): F *beetles*. The origin of *beetle* in this sense as a verb appears to be its occurrence as a nonce-word in the Folio. I have therefore retained the Q 2 reading. See O.E.D.

I. iv. 82. *arture*; the Q 2 reading retained (F *artire*; both are old spellings of *artery*, the usual reading) to mark the less usual use of it as equivalent to 'ligament.'

I. v. 68. *possess*; so Q 2. The F reading *posset* has been almost universally adopted. At first sight it is very tempting, but there is a certain redundance in the repetition of the 'curd' metaphor, and the movement from the general 'possession' (to which the *sudden vigour* is appropriate enough) to the specific *curd* is quite effective.

I. v. 136. *by St. Patrick*; perhaps St. Patrick rather than any other saint because of his connection with snakes, *cf.* ll. 36, 39 above.

I. v. 173. *encumber'd*; Q 2 reads *incombred*. I suspect, lurking below this, 'akimbo' in one of its old forms, e.g. *on kembow* or *in kenebowe*. If Shakespeare could have spelt either of those with a *c* for the *k* there would be graphically little difficulty in the corruption.

I. v. 178. The reading of Q 2, which is quite grammatical, is retained. But both F and Q 1 read

> *this not to do,*
> *So grace and mercy at your most need help you,*
> *Swear*

and on the stage the picking up of the *never shall* in l. 172 no doubt makes things easier.

II. i. 52. A pretty instance of the F insertion. The F reviser is trying to make this passage square exactly with l. 46, and does not see that in Q 2 Reynaldo does in fact give Polonius the cue he needs, as Polonius recognises in l. 54, and that giving him the insignificant 'friend' and 'gentleman' will not help him at all.

II. i. 118. A meaning can be extracted, 'if I keep Hamlet's love hidden the hiding it may cause more grief than the disclosure may cause resentment'; but *hate* is an oddly strong word, and the grammatical construction of *love* is awkward; I feel that there is probably some corruption.

II. ii. 90. *Therefore, for brevity*; Q 2 reads *Therefore brevity*. F fills in the gap with *since*. I rather prefer *for* as a more natural omission for the Q compositor. But for sense (apart from metre) we are as well without either.

II. ii. 182. *good kissing carrion*; so both Q 2 and F. The usual emendation, *god kissing carrion*, has much to commend it, particularly in that it maintains the rhetorical balance of the sentence; but the text as it stands is interpretable enough, so long as we realise that it means 'carrion good for kissing' (*i.e.* to be kissed). (*Cf.* 'a good acting play.')

II. ii. 333. This remark, and the long 'F only' passage which follows, have been the occasion of long comment and dispute,

HAMLET

which cannot be adequately summarised. Is the 'inhibition,' for example, an actual inhibition, caused by (a) the plague of 1603, or (b) a period of disgrace of Shakespeare's company in 1601, or does it merely mean a period of unpopularity caused by the popularity of a new company of child actors (1600-1)? The matter is of much greater importance for the history of the stage than for the play of *Hamlet*.

II. ii. 378. *handsaw*; a corruption (not necessarily the compositor's) of *hernshaw* (*i.e.* 'heron') in the correct form of the proverb.

II. ii. 558. *her*; so Q 2. Q 1 and F read *Hecuba*. The Q 2 reading may be merely a misunderstanding of a contracted *Hec*.

III. i. 13. It is tempting to transpose *Niggard* and *Most free*; but there is no justification for the transposition, and we must just suppose that Rosencrantz and Guildenstern have been completely bewildered.

III. i. 109. *converse*; F reads *commerce*, which may be right, but Q 2's *comerse* is only a minim error for *converse*.

III. i. 160, 161. F reads *tune* and *feature*, which are the generally accepted readings. They are graphically quite possible, but I see no convincing reason for abandoning Q 2.

III. ii. 71. *commedled*; an interesting case of F alteration. *Commeddled* is a good enough word, and used by Webster in *The White Devil*; but less usual than the *commingled* which F reads.

III. ii. 165-67. Thus Q 2. Something is wrong, since the first line has no rhyme and the third is hypermetric. A line has probably dropped out, unless the passage was left unfinished. It has fairly clearly been under correction, since the third line looks as though it had originally started *In either none* (to be continued *or in extremity*), which had been cancelled in favour of *in neither ought*, and the compositor had neglected most of the cancellation.

III. ii. 264. *What, frighted with false fire?* So F (Q 1 *fires*), and a curious omission for the Q 2 compositor to make if he had the words in front of him. Nor do I think the remark in itself as simple as, from a general silence, it presumably appears to most commentators. When it is commented on at all, it is usually in such words as " *i.e.* by a mere play." But that is surely the oddest possible comment for Hamlet to make, when the whole design of the play has been to present to the King something so close to the truth that he will give himself away, and to make at a moment when the design has brilliantly succeeded. I suggest rather tentatively that what Hamlet had intended as his climax, the speech of a dozen or sixteen lines, for which critics have so diligently hunted, was to do not with the murder, but with the marriage of Gonzago's wife ("*you shall see anon how* . . ."), and has not yet come : and that Hamlet is exasperated, because the King has gone off at half-cock, and so spoiled his artistic climax.

III. ii. 282. *pacock*; Q 2 and F both read *paiocke*, commonly in modern texts given as *pajock*; a word which has produced a wealth of comment, one commentator enlivening the aridity of the discussion by the despairing suggestion that the word is a stage-direction for a hiccup. The reading here is the suggestion of Dover Wilson, and seems entirely acceptable. It is a normal form of ' peacock,' whereas *pajock* is very dubious ; and graphically the corruption to *paiocke* is easy. But we should perhaps notice that Spenser uses *patchocke* for a clown, and this would easily be mistaken, in hearing, though not in writing, for *pajock*.

III. ii. 353. *thumbs*; Q 2 *the umber*, F *thumb*; doubtless correct so far, but improved by Dover Wilson to the plural, which accounts for the *r* of *umber*.

III. iii. 6, 7. *lunacies*; so F. Q 2 reads *browes*. The F emendation, apart from graphical difficulties, is awkward metrically. D. Wilson suggests *brawls* or *braues*, I prefer the second.

III. iii. 79. *hire and salary*; so F. Q 2 reads *base and silly*. This is clearly nonsense; but equally clearly it could hardly be a misreading of something which could be read correctly as *hire and salary*. Q 1 reads *this is a benefit, And not . . .* It is just worth observing that *nefitt*, followed by one of the forms of ampersand, could easily be read as *nd sill y*, though it is harder to extract *is base a* from *is a be*, unless *sabe* got read as *base*.

III. iv. 48–51. This is the Q 2 reading. F tried to improve matters by putting a stop at *glow*, reading *Yea* for *O'er* and *tristful* for *heated*, but though this improves the grammar it is more than doubtful whether it improves the sense; to give the *solidity and compound mass* a visage, either *tristful* or *heated*, seems to me awkward, whereas the picture of Heaven looking down with glowing, heated face seems natural enough. I suspect the corruption of lying in *as against the doom* which has hitherto passed almost unchallenged, except by Warburton, who read *and as 'gainst . . .*, which gives very tolerable sense.

III. iv. 161. The easiest emendation of this passage is to omit (with Q 2) the comma after *eat*, and read (with Theobald-Thirlby) *evil* for *devil*.

III. iv. 194. The ape presumably, having seen the birds fly out of the basket, tried to imitate them, got into the basket, jumped out of it, fell from the house-top, and broke his neck; but the story is lost.

IV. ii. 18. *like an ape*; so F. Q 2 reads *like an apple*, and the reading of Q1, *as an ape doth nuttes*, suggests that what the ape keeps was indicated, and gives some probability to Farmer's conjecture *like an ape an apple*.

IV. iii. 68. *will ne'er begin*; so Q 2. F completes the expected couplet, but with awkward syntax, *were ne'er begun.*

IV. iv. 25-26. The silence of the commentators suggests that they find these lines easy. But since Hamlet's whole point is that lives and wealth *will* be expended in debating the question, he seems to say the opposite of what one expects. Either we must force 'debate' to mean 'suffice to settle,' or we must emend (? *now* for *not*).

IV. iv. 54. This is often explained to mean that true greatness will not stir without great argument, but that it finds such great argument in a straw when honour is at stake. But I think it is much more probably one of those frequent instances in Shakespeare where there is a confusion with negatives, and that its real meaning is that which is assumed by nine out of ten casual and rapid readers, *i.e.* ' true greatness is not to refuse to stir (not not to stir) without . . .'

IV. v. S.D. F gets rid of an extra actor by discarding the *Gentleman* altogether and giving his speeches to Horatio.

IV. v. 158. *old man's life*; so F, and it is the contrast needed; but it is difficult to see how Q 2's reading of *poore* for *old* arose, and Q 1's reading, *young maid's life* and *old man's sawe*, suggest that the passage was in some confusion.

IV. vii. 68-81. An interesting case of F joining the flats. It reads *And call it accident. Some two months since.*

V. i. 9. *so offended*; emendation is always extremely perilous when the speeches are those of characters part of whose humour consists in verbal blunders. Q 2 reads *so offended*, and F *se offendendo*; but it is rash to assume that the double blunder for *se defendendo* is the compositor's and not the clown's.

V. i. 61. *get thee in, and fetch*; so Q 2; the F reading is the well-known *get thee to Yaughan; fetch.* If Yaughan, as is generally supposed, was a nearby inn-keeper, the allusion is the kind of topical one that might be introduced as an effective gag at any period of the play's history. One ought to add that Q 1 reads *get thee gone*, which might be a mishearing of *get thee to Yaughan*.

V. i. 103-12. Shakespeare, as often, is punning on legal terminology. The technicalities are concerned with land tenure, and hardly worth giving in detail.

V. ii. 136-40. Here again we can see the F reviser at work. He cuts as the brackets indicate: but then he sees that Hamlet's *What's his weapon* is left hanging in the air: so he reads before his cut *You are not ignorant of what excellence Laertes is at his weapon*.

V. ii. 179-85. This passage is given substantially as in F, since Q 2 has made such a botch of it that some emendation must be admitted. (Q 2 reads *sir* for *comply*, *out of an* for *outward*, *histy* for *yesty*, *prophane and trennowed* for *fond and winnowed*. But Q 2 probably conceals an original other and more comprehensible than the version of F, even though the original is now irrecoverable.)

V. ii. 205. *gain-giving*; so F. Q 2 reads *gamgiving*. The F emendation is graphically as easy as possible, but results in an awkward nonce-word for *misgiving*. One can hardly escape suspecting a concealed *qualm*.

V. ii. 212. *since no man of aught . . . let be*; so Q 2 (with spelling *ought* and a comma after *leaves*). F reads *since no man ha's ought of what he leaues. What is't to leaue betimes?* There has been much dispute and conjecture, mostly coloured by the question-mark of F. But Dover Wilson excellently points out that Q 2 makes good sense as it stands so soon as we remember that *is't* can stand for the affirmative *'tis* or *it is* as well as the interrogative *is it?*

V. ii. (213) S.D. The directions of both Q 2 and F are given, since one difference (the *daggers* of Q 2) has some importance in the hotly debated question of the interchange of rapiers.

V. ii. 234-36. Laertes takes up both Hamlet's points of 'nature' and 'honour.' He means 'my inclination is certainly for forgiveness, so long as I can be assured by experts that I shall not stain my honour.'

V. ii. 277. *fat*; the trouble over this word seems to be resolved by the account given by a trio of American schoolboys of their reception, while hiking on a very hot day, at a Middle Western farmhouse. They asked for a drink of water. "Sure," said the farmer's wife, "come in and sit down; you're all so fat." "Fat?" said they, somewhat insulted. "Why," said she, "it's dripping off you." She meant simply 'sweating', with no allusion to their figures. Hence, in the present passage, the Queen's offer of a napkin. And cf. Falstaff 'larding' the lean earth. (I had this, in casual conversation, from an American professor, who had had it at first hand, but whose name I have unhappily forgotten, and to whom, if it has since appeared in print over his name, I owe my apologies for the lack of formal acknowledgment. I should add that the story was rounded off by the statement—not gone bail for—that the farmer's wife's forbears had come from Warwickshire!).

V. ii. (292) S.D. This stage direction is Rowe's, a combination of Q 1 (*They catch one another's rapiers, and both are wounded*) and F (*In scuffling they change rapiers*). Q 2 unhelpfully gives no S.D. at all. There has been much long and technical argument as to the method of the change. The one point which is perfectly clear is that they must actually change, since there is only one unbated and envenomed foil. That Laertes, after wounding Hamlet, is disarmed, and Hamlet gives his own foil to Laertes and picks up his, is as simple as any.

V. ii. 373. *forc'd*; so F, correcting Q 2's *for no*. Possibly *feign'd* (spelled *faind*).

Glossary

MANY words and phrases in Shakespeare require glossing, not because they are in themselves unfamiliar, but for the opposite reason, that Shakespeare uses in their Elizabethan and unfamiliar sense a large number of words which seem so familiar that there is no incentive to look for them in the glossary. It is hoped that a glossary arranged as below will make it easy to see at a glance what words and phrases in any particular scene require elucidation. A number of phrases are glossed by what seems to be, in their context, the modern equivalent rather than by lexicographical glosses on the words which compose them.

Act First

SCENE I

line

13 RIVALS, partners
57 SENSIBLE AND TRUE AVOUCH OF MINE OWN EYES, certain witness of my sense of sight
65 JUMP, exactly
68 GROSS AND SCOPE, general range
72 SUBJECT, *collective sing. for plur.*
89 SEIZ'D OF, possessed of
94 CARRIAGE, terms
   DESIGN'D, drawn up
96 UNIMPROVED, unproved (?)

line

107 ROMAGE, hurly-burly
125 CLIMATURES, regions (?)
134 HAPPILY, haply
140 PARTISAN, spear with cutting blade
154 EXTRAVAGANT, wandering beyond its appointed bounds
   ERRING, errant
162 STRIKE, blast
163 TAKES, charms (malignantly)

SCENE II

9 JOINTRESS, widow with a jointure, dowager
10 DEFEATED, marred

38 DELATED, conveyed to you
45 LOSE YOUR VOICE, waste your breath

Act I Sc. ii—*continued*

line

47 NATIVE, akin

70 VAILED, lowered (*not the same as 'veiled'*)

92 OBSEQUIOUS, to do with obsequies

93 CONDOLEMENT, lamentation

95 TO, in sight of, (*or simply*) towards

99 VULGAR, commonplace

107 UNPREVAILING, unavailing

127 ROUSE, bumper

137 POSSESS IT MERELY, are its only occupants

140 HYPERION, the Sun-god

141 BETEEM, permit

147 OR ERE, before

line

149 NIOBE, her children were killed by Apollo and Artemis, and as she wept for them she turned to stone

150 DISCOURSE, faculty

155 FLUSHING, redness

182 DEAREST FOE, 'bosom-enemy'

192 SEASON, moderate
ADMIRATION, wonder

200 AT POINT, in readiness
CAP-A-PE, head to foot

204 TRUNCHEON, baton, (*or*) shaft of spear

205 ACT, operation

216 IT, its

229 BEAVER, visor of helmet

SCENE III

3 CONVOY IS ASSISTANT, means of transport is ready

6 FASHION, mere mood
TOY IN BLOOD, passing desire

7 PRIMY, spring-like

9 SUPPLIANCE, amusement

15 SOIL, stain
CAUTEL, deceit

23 YIELDING, consent

40 BUTTONS, buds

45 EFFECT, gist

51 REDE, advice

69 CENSURE, opinion

81 SEASON, (*three possible meanings*) ripen, preserve, make palatable

83 TEND, wait

94 PUT ON ME, reported to me

96 UNDERSTAND YOURSELF, 'know your place'

102 UNSIFTED, untried

112 FASHION, fancy (*passing*)

115 SPRINGES, traps

122 ENTREATMENTS, interviews

128 INVESTMENTS, *pun on two senses*

SCENE IV

line

9 UP-SPRING, riotous dance
19 CLEPE, call
20 SOIL OUR ADDITION, give us a bad name
22 ATTRIBUTE, deserved reputation
28 PALES, palisades
30 PLAUSIVE, praiseworthy
38 HIS, its

line

43 QUESTIONABLE, demanding question
47 CANONIZ'D, buried with the rites
83 NEMEAN LION, killed by Hercules
NERVE, sinew
85 LETS, hinders

SCENE V

21 ETERNAL BLAZON, account of the other world
37 PROCESS, account
52 TO, compared with
61 SECURE, care-free
62 HEBONA, ? henbane
69 EAGER, acid
71 TETTER, eruption
72 LAZAR-LIKE, leper-like
77 UNHOUSEL'D, without sacrament
DISAPPOINTED, unprepared
UNANNEL'D, unanointed
83 LUXURY, lust

94 INSTANT, *adv.*
97 GLOBE, *probably* head, *but possibly with allusion to* microcosm
98 TABLE, tablet
99 FOND, foolish
100 PRESSURES, imprints
136 SAINT PATRICK, perhaps because of his traditional connection with serpents; see l. 39
167 YOUR PHILOSOPHY, philosophy in general
172 ANTIC, fantastic

Act Second

SCENE I

8 KEEP, lodge
10 ENCOMPASSMENT AND DRIFT OF QUESTION, round about method of questioning
20 FORGERIES, inventions
31 QUAINTLY, ingeniously

35 OF GENERAL ASSAULT, 'a thing that might happen to anyone'
38 FETCH OF WARRANT, guaranteed (*or* justifiable) device

Act II Sc. i—*continued*

line

45 CLOSES WITH YOU IN THIS CON-
    SEQUENCE, replies as follows

47 ADDITION, style of address

58 ROUSE, carousing

64 WINDLASSES, circuitous ap-
    proaches (*met. from hunting*)
    ASSAYS OF BIAS, trials of bias
    (*met. from bowls*)

line

79 DOWN-GYVED, having slipped
    down till they were like
    fetters

101 ECSTASY, madness

102 PROPERTY, quality

111 COTED, observed

114 CAST BEYOND OURSELVES, over-
    shoot the mark

SCENE II

2 MOREOVER THAT, beyond the fact
    that

6 SITH, since

7 THAT, what

12 HAVIOUR, behaviour

22 GENTRY, courtesy

67 BORNE IN HAND, deluded

79 REGARDS OF SAFETY AND ALLOW-
    ANCE, terms of permission as
    will guarantee your safety

86 EXPOSTULATE, discuss

136 TABLE-BOOK, memorandum-book

141 OUT OF THY STAR, in a different
    (social) sphere

142 PRESCRIPTS, orders

149 LIGHTNESS, light-headedness

159 CENTRE, *i.e.* of the earth

165 THEREON, as a result

168 SADLY, seriously

170 BOARD, 'tackle'
    GIVE ME LEAVE, leave me (*a
    polite request*)

228 INDIFFERENT, ordinary

265 OUTSTRETCH'D, (*meaning doubt-
    ful*); straining every nerve (?)

271 MAKE YOU, are you doing

286 CONSONANCY, harmony

287 OBLIGATION, binding power

303 FRETTED, 'criss-crossed'

307 EXPRESS, well-adapted

319 COTED, overtook (Q I reads
    boarded)

324 HUMOROUS MAN, (*not the mod-
    ern sense*); *either just* fanciful,
    or perhaps the actor who
    played the 'humours'

326 TICKLE O' THE SERE, 'hair-
    triggerish' (*like a fire-arm that
    is light in the pull and is liable
    to go off on the least provocation*)

340 EYASES, young hawks

341 ON THE TOP OF QUESTION,
    drowning criticism

344 GOOSE-QUILLS, (the satirical) pens
    (of those writing plays for the
    children)

Act II   Sc. ii—*continued*

Act Third

SCENE I

Act III   Sc. i—*continued*

line

76 BODKIN, dagger
   FARDELS, packs
79 BOURN, frontier
83 CONSCIENCE, habit of reasoning
86 OF GREAT PITCH AND MOMENT, of momentous importance
87 WITH THIS REGARD, because this is reflected on

line

118 INOCULATE, graft new stock on to
    RELISH, keep a strain of
161 BLOWN, in full bloom
162 ECSTASY, madness
164 AFFECTIONS, state of mind
167 ON BROOD, brooding
177 FASHION OF HIMSELF, his usual self
185 ROUND, blunt

SCENE II

20 MODESTY, moderation
21 FROM, alien from
26 PRESSURE, imprint
28 OF WHICH ONE, of one of whom
29 ALLOWANCE, estimation
35 JOURNEYMEN, inferior craftsmen
36 ABHOMINABLY, *a pun on the* ab homine *derivation*
37 INDIFFERENTLY, more or less
50 PRESENTLY, at once
62 CANDIED, sugary
63 PREGNANT, ready
71 COMMEDLED, mingled
83 IN, on the occasion of
86 STITHY, smithy
89 CENSURE OF, judgement on
92 IDLE, 'daft'
117 COUNTRY, 'rude'
125 JIG-MAKER, see II. ii. 499
130 SABLES, *with a pun on the two senses,* furs, *and* black
138 MICHING MALLECHO, skulking mischief (?)

146 YOU ARE NAUGHT, 'I am not amused'
150 POSY, motto
153 PHŒBUS, the Sun-god
154 NEPTUNE, the Ocean-god
    TELLUS, the Earth
166 QUANTITY, proportion
181 INSTANCES, motives
182 RESPECTS, considerations
208 SEASONS HIM, ripens him into
218 ANCHOR'S, anchorite
219 BLANKS THE FACE OF JOY, puts joy out of countenance
236 TROPICALLY, figuratively (*in the Eliz. pronunciation there is a pun on* 'trap')
273 FEATHERS, *were much used on the stage for ornaments*
274 TURN TURK, make a complete change (as from Christian to infidel)
    PROVINCIAL ROSES, rosettes (*imitating the Rose de Provence*)

191

Act III   Sc. ii—*continued*

line
275 RAZ'D, 'slashed'
276 CRY, company
289 RECORDERS, a kind of flute (held vertically)
322 AMAZEMENT AND ADMIRATION, bewilderment and wonder
340 WITHDRAW WITH YOU, speak to you aside
341 RECOVER THE WIND OF ME, get to windward of (*i.e.* to frighten the deer in the opposite direction)

line
342 TOIL, snare
351 TOUCH, fingering (of a musical instrument)
352 VENTAGES, holes
366 FRET, equip with frets (*i.e.* the cross-bars on which the strings of a lute are stopped)
370 PRESENTLY, at once
392 SHENT, blamed

SCENE III

7 BRAVES, wild behaviour
7 PROVIDE, prepare
11 PECULIAR, individual
15 CEASE, cessation
16 GULF, whirlpool
22 RUIN, downfall
29 THE PROCESS, what occurs
33 OF VANTAGE, from a favourable position; (*or perhaps simply*) in addition

64 GIVE IN, produce
69 ENGAG'D, closely stuck
75 WOULD BE SCANN'D, needs to be examined
81 FLUSH, lusty
88 HENT, (*meaning doubtful*); grasp, *or* design, *or* for 'hint,' occasion

SCENE IV

38 SENSE, feeling
46 FROM THE BODY OF CONTRACTION PLUCKS THE VERY SOUL, makes all contracts valueless
52 INDEX, table of contents at *beginning* of a book
71 SENSE, perception
72 MOTION, emotion

77 HOODMAN-BLIND, blindman's buff
81 MOPE, be insensitive
90 GRAINED, ingrained
92 ENSEAMED, loaded with grease
98 PRECEDENT, former
98 VICE, the comic figure in the old interludes and moralities
108 IMPORTANT, urgent

Act III   Sc. iv—*continued*

line
114 CONCEIT, fancy
121 EXCREMENTS, outgrowths (i.e. *as though the outgrowths had life of their own*)
127 CAPABLE, *i.e.* of sensation
151 COMPOST, manure

line
182 BLOWT, bloated
184 REECHY, rancid
188 IN CRAFT, as a trick
190 PADDOCK, toad
     GIB, cat
207 PETAR, mortar (explosive)

Act Fourth

SCENE I

11 BRAINISH APPREHENSION, head-strong fancy
16 ANSWER'D, given account of
18 KEPT SHORT, kept in check

18 OUT OF HAUNT, isolated
25 ORE, precious metal
26 MINERAL, mine
42 BLANK, mark

SCENE II

16 OFFICERS, servants

30 HIDE FOX, AND ALL AFTER, the 'hide-and-seek' signal

SCENE III

7 BEAR, keep
48 CHERUB, the cherubim were angels specifically of knowledge

54 AT FOOT, at his heels
62 SET, esteem
66 HECTIC, fever

SCENE IV

15 MAIN, main strength
16 FRONTIER, border town
22 RANKER, greater
   IN FEE, freehold
27 IMPOSTHUME, abscess
34 HIS CHIEF GOOD AND MARKET OF HIS TIME, the best that he does with his time

36 LARGE DISCOURSE, power of wide-ranging reflection
39 FUST, grow fusty (*i.e.* tasting of the cask)
47 CHARGE, cost
61 TRICK OF FAME, trifle of reputation
64 CONTINENT, anything that contains

SCENE V

line

6 SPURNS ENVIOUSLY AT STRAWS, *probably metaphorical*, is peevish at trifles

8 UNSHAPED USE, disconnectedness

9 COLLECTION, deduce sense for it

18 TOY, trifle

19 ARTLESS JEALOUSY, causeless suspicion

25 COCKLE HAT, hat with pilgrim's cockle-shell

40 'ILD, yield (*i.e.* reward)

51 DUPP'D, do up = open

56 BY GIS, by Jesus

81 GREENLY, foolishly

87 IN CLOUDS, gloomy

93 MURDERING-PIECE, small cannon firing canister

94 SUPERFLUOUS DEATH, *i.e.* many mortal wounds

97 LIST, limit (*cf.* lists)

108 COUNTER, 'hunting counter' is

line

following the scent in the wrong direction

117 HERE, at this moment

123 HIS, its

140 SWOOPSTAKE, taking the whole stake at once; *i.e.* indiscriminately

145 REPAST, feed

160 INSTANCE, token

176 DOCUMENT, lesson

178 FENNEL, *for flattery* COLUMBINES, *for faithlessness*

179 RUE, *for repentance*

180-181 WEAR . . . WITH A DIFFERENCE, (*in the heraldic sense; almost*) with a different implication

118 DAISY, *for deceit*

182 VIOLETS, *for faithfulness*

211 TROPHY, emblem on a tomb HATCHMENT, tablet with armorial bearings

SCENE VI

25 BORE, calibre

SCENE VII

1 CONSCIENCE, cognisance of the facts

7 CAPITAL, (*as in*) 'capital' charge

14 CONJUNCTIVE, closely connected with

17 COUNT, trial

18 GENERAL GENDER, common people

22 TOO SLIGHTLY TIMBER'D, with shafts too light

Act IV   Sc. vii—*continued*

line
28 ON MOUNT, above
67 UNCHARGE, not suspect
70 ORGAN, instrument
76 SIEGE, rank
84 CAN WELL, are experts
89 FORGERY, inventing
100 SCRIMERS, fencers
117 PLURISY, plethora
138 UNBATED, without the 'button'
143 CATAPLASM, plaster

line
154 BLAST IN PROOF, crack when being tested
167 ASCAUNT, aslant
173 CRONET, in form of a coronet
178 LAUDS, hymns
179 INCAPABLE OF, not comprehending
180 INDUED UNTO, fitted to live in
190 THE WOMAN WILL BE OUT, my feminine weakness will be ended
192 DOUTS, puts out

Act Fifth

SCENE I

12 ARGAL, *blunder for* ergo
34 ARMS, *pun on the two senses*
68 PROPERTY OF EASINESS, easy habit
79 O'ER-REACHES, gets the better of
89 MAZZARD, head
92 LOGGITS, a kind of quoits
99 QUIDDITIES, quibbles
QUILLETS, subtleties
106 FINE, end
138 BY THE CARD, (*originally* the card of the compass, *and hence*) precisely
141 PICK'D, 'refaned'
143 KIBE, chilblain
166 POCKY, infected with the pox (*i.e.* syphilis)

196 FAVOUR, appearance
212 LOAM, plaster
217 FLAW, gust of wind
229 ORDER, regular procedure
233 CRANTS, wreaths
234 STREWMENTS, flowers strewn
254 PELION, a high mountain in Thessaly. *The giants in the war against the Olympian deities 'piled Pelion on Ossa' to reach their enemies. See line 284 below*
277 ESILL, vinegar
283 BURNING ZONE, sun's course
288 GOLDEN COUPLETS, twin (*yellow*) fledglings
296 PRESENT PUSH, immediate trial

HAMLET

SCENE II

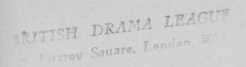